Nice Guys Finish Last
and Other Workplace Lies

Nice Guys Finish Last and Other Workplace Lies

Successfully Navigating the Modern Workplace

John Ruffa

Nice Guys Finish Last and Other Workplace Lies:
Successfully Navigating the Modern Workplace

Copyright © John Ruffa, 2024

Cover design by Brent Beckley and John Ruffa

Interior design by Exeter Premedia Services Private Ltd., Chennai, India

All rights reserved. No part of this publication may be reproduced, stored in a retrieval system, or transmitted in any form or by any means—electronic, mechanical, photocopy, recording, or any other except for brief quotations, not to exceed 400 words, without the prior permission of the publisher.

First published in 2024 by
Business Expert Press, LLC
222 East 46th Street, New York, NY 10017
www.businessexpertpress.com

ISBN-13: 978-1-63742-732-3 (paperback)
ISBN-13: 978-1-63742-733-0 (e-book)

Business Expert Press Service Human Resource Management and Organizational Behavior Collection

First edition: 2024

10 9 8 7 6 5 4 3 2 1

To my good friend Ken, who first encouraged me to write this book and walked alongside me throughout the entire process. Without your constant help and encouragement along the way, this book would have never happened. I'm extremely grateful for friends like you.

To my amazing wife and kids, who often endured long hours when I was away at work developing NASA missions—you are my greatest gift and make my life a true adventure! Always watch out for S-NASA!

To Mike, my mentor, sounding board, and good friend over these many years—thanks for all you taught me and the example you continually set. Your fingerprints are all over these pages.

And finally, to the many valued co-workers and faithful friends who I had the immense privilege of working with over my career—there are too many of you to name, but you know who you are! You were the key to any success I had, and always made me look smarter and more capable than I actually was. You will always be part of my valued community.

Description

Today's modern workplace can be an extremely challenging place. Virtually everyone has a story about an impossible boss, a difficult co-worker, a challenging deadline, a toxic work environment, a lack of resources, and an annoying new policy—leaving today's workers in serious need of trusted advice to navigate the daily challenges they face.

Unfortunately, much of the advice circulating in today's workplace is misleading and untrue, full of rarely challenged and generally accepted principles and "truths" that are actually false. Regrettably, well-meaning people often adopt these lies, myths, and misrepresentations and too often suffer the consequences of the poor advice that they convey.

Nice Guys Finish Last and Other Workplace Lies: Successfully Navigating the Modern Workplace meets this urgent need by serving as an essential resource for today's workers. It directly identifies and exposes the lies, half-truths, and misperceptions that cause havoc and disruption in the workplace, offering time-tested principles addressing workplace challenges and facilitating workplace success and advancement.

Written by an experienced NASA engineer with a long career of practical, hands-on experience leading technical teams on complex spaceflight missions, this book leverages years of experience to clearly identify the lies and mistruths prevalent in today's workforce. Armed with a wealth of examples from his own challenging workplace experiences, each chapter identifies common workplace falsehoods and highlights key principles vital for workplace success.

Written in a straightforward, entertaining, and easy-to-digest manner, *Nice Guys Finish Last and Other Workplace Lies* dispels commonly accepted workplace myths and provides the reader with the benefits of a lifetime of practical workplace experiences without having to experience the "school of hard knocks" themselves.

Contents

Foreword xi

Chapter 1   Lies in the Workplace 1
Chapter 2   Technical Versus Non-Technical Challenges 9
Chapter 3   The Need for "Soft Skills" in a "Hard Skill" World 13
Chapter 4   Building Your Community 19
Chapter 5   A Failure to Communicate 23
Chapter 6   The Value of a Mentor 29
Chapter 7   What, Me a Mentor? 37
Chapter 8   You Have to Earn It 41
Chapter 9   Drawing the Line 47
Chapter 10   Crawl Before You Walk, Walk Before You Run 53
Chapter 11   Wherever You Go, There You Are 59
Chapter 12   Climbing Out of the Ivory Tower 67
Chapter 13   I Can't Hear What You're Saying, Your Actions Are Speaking Too Loudly 71
Chapter 14   Creating a Team Culture 77
Chapter 15   The Danger of No Dissent 83
Chapter 16   Reinventing the Wheel 87
Chapter 17   The Right Man (or Woman) for the Job 91
Chapter 18   Training Your Replacement 95
Chapter 19   Someone Looking Over Your Shoulder 101
Chapter 20   Are You Better Off With Them or Without Them? 107
Chapter 21   Are You an Impostor? 113
Chapter 22   The Big Red Line 119
Chapter 23   Avoiding Blind Spots 123
Chapter 24   The Value of Worry 129
Chapter 25   Risky Business 133
Chapter 26   Breaking the Rules 137
Chapter 27   Recovering From Failure 143

Chapter 28	The Art of Negotiation	151
Chapter 29	Fear Versus Loyalty	155
Chapter 30	Don't Let Things Roll Downhill	161
Chapter 31	No Stupid Questions Allowed	167
Chapter 32	Seeing the Big Picture	171
Chapter 33	Setting Boundaries	177
Chapter 34	Burning Out	181
Chapter 35	Sometimes the Problem Is Just Hard	187
Chapter 36	Voting With Your Feet	191
Chapter 37	Treating People Right	197
Chapter 38	Being a Lifelong Learner	201
Chapter 39	The Value of Experience	205
Chapter 40	Avoiding Communication Missteps	209
Chapter 41	The Value of Relationships	215
Chapter 42	Next Steps	221

About the Author 223
Index 225

Foreword

Over the course of my nearly 40-year career, I feel I've done almost every technical job imaginable, starting at the bottom and slowly working my way up through roles of progressively greater responsibility. I started off at the beginning of my career as an electronics designer, working on R&D projects. When I moved on to NASA, I started as a product development lead responsible for leading a team of skilled designers in the conceptualization, design, manufacture, test, and delivery of state-of-the-art spacecraft avionics systems. I later moved up to a systems engineering role, where I led the development and execution of comprehensive tests for advanced NASA spacecraft to ensure that they were ready for launch. I've sat on flight operations consoles leading the successful launch and in-orbit checkout of NASA missions, and I've been called in late at night to help diagnose and recover from on-orbit spacecraft anomalies. All these experiences ultimately led me to become a missions systems engineer, the highest technical role on a NASA mission. In this senior role, I led the entire mission project technical team through the development and launch of our mission, as well as serving as the Engineering Technical Authority to ensure that everything was executed correctly with no mistakes or missteps. In addition to all this, I've also served on spacecraft review teams and worked at the NASA program level to help other mission development efforts. Along the way, I've mentored aspiring systems engineers, where I passed on my hard-won lessons-learned. I've had an amazing career, doing things that I only dreamed of as a youngster who grew up during the Apollo era.

My work and that of the countless other skilled people I've worked alongside is significant because of what NASA does. We labor diligently to build high-tech and high-reliability spacecraft that will work and not fail. This is much harder than most people think. A faulty spacecraft cannot be brought back for repair if it has problems after launch—it has to work right the first time. On top of this, we have to meet challenging launch dates (often on a limited budget), adding a significant amount of pressure to the endeavor. Missing a launch date not only adds extra cost but, for some missions, the next launch opportunity may not come for weeks or months (or even longer for planetary missions!) because of flight trajectory parameters. All this might sound stressful and intimidating (and it often is!), but the exhilaration of seeing your work return valuable science data is indescribable.

When I look back over my career, as successful as I was, I could never have accomplished this without the many positive working relationships I developed with others across all positions and technical disciplines. During my career, I've worked alongside and learned from some of the most brilliant and talented people imaginable. Over time and many missions, I've seen what makes projects and their teams successful and what causes them to struggle (and even fail). These types of missions can be extremely high-pressure and place those working on them under a tremendous amount of stress. It's tempting, under these conditions, to resort to autocratic or aggressive tactics with co-workers to try to force things along in order to make much-needed progress. I was certainly tempted at times. However, I discovered that being collaborative and treating others with respect was always the best way to get the job done. I always believed that the way we treat other people matters, and treating people with respect shouldn't be compromised in order to make progress. While I was not always perfect in holding this standard across my long career, I am glad that I maintained my values throughout.

That's what this book is about—passing on these hard-won lessons-learned that served me so well over my long career, hopefully so that others might benefit from them. Many of these lessons reflect leadership principles taught in other places. Some might consider them "common sense" principles. What I feel makes them true is that, although they might be simple, they were work- and people-tested many times in the crucible of the NASA environment. Their power comes from faithfully applying them and seeing them work.

As you read this book, I hope you'll gain an appreciation of these simple truths and apply them to your career as I did so that you are better able to navigate today's complex workplace environment.

CHAPTER 1

Lies in the Workplace

Nice guys finish last.

This statement represents a widely accepted axiom in today's workplace. Countless workers, hoping to succeed in the job market, have based their entire careers and workplace behavior on this premise. They often compromise their personal values and beliefs on the idea that "being nice" means that they will be hindered in their workplace success and will hurt their chances for advancement and achievement. "Nice guys finish last" is often used as an excuse for compromising one's personal ethics and resorting to unethical, underhanded, duplicitous, and otherwise questionable behavior in order to "get ahead." Any twinge from an uneasy conscience is often dismissed with the excuse that "everybody does it."

There's just one problem. This generally accepted "truth" is actually a lie.

While it is true that being duplicitous, underhanded, unkind, and unethical in your workplace dealings *can* actually allow you to advance more rapidly than others in the short term, this is typically *not* true for the long haul. By lying about inconvenient facts and results, taking credit for someone else's work, or engaging in other questionable workplace practices that give you an unfair (and unethical) advantage over your co-workers, it *is* possible to use this unfair advantage as a short-term stepping stone to rise more rapidly than others around you. People who employ such dubious tactics may even get away with it for a while. However, what advocates of this philosophy don't tell you is that any "success" built on this dubious foundation is essentially a house of cards. Unlike a career and reputation that is built on a firm foundation of hard work and ethical behavior (and the resulting good reputation that these admirable characteristics typically yield), a rickety career structure based on unethical conduct has the potential to collapse at any moment, often with catastrophic results. Even a brief examination of the daily news regularly highlights individuals whose questionable workplace practices eventually come to light and are exposed, often resulting in the shipwreck of their careers and reputation. Even if any compromises and misdeeds don't eventually come to light through public exposure, the personal burden of maintaining a façade to hide unethical or unkind behavior toward others can be its own punishment.

Early in my engineering technical career, before I started to work at NASA, I once worked for a man who we'll call "Fred." Fred was seen as a rising star in our organization. He was truly talented and skilled and began to rapidly advance, surpassing his peers. Things looked very bright for Fred's long-term future. But then, something changed. I'm not sure when it happened, but, somewhere, Fred decided that his rapid rise was just not fast enough. He apparently bought into the adage that "nice guys finish last"—and that getting ahead more quickly meant that he needed to start adopting practices that, frankly, weren't very nice. I had a front row seat to Fred's evolving leadership approach and how it unfolded in the day-to-day operation of his team. He started engaging in increasingly questionable behavior, such as claiming credit for accomplishments that the entire group worked hard to achieve, bullying those working under his leadership in an attempt to meet difficult project deadlines, and engaging in quiet criticism campaigns against perceived rivals to make himself look better. To those like me who had a front row seat to these behavioral changes, Fred quickly developed the characteristics of an uncompromising and abusive leader, pushing his employees through manipulative and intimidating tactics. Even when his employees met his stringent and difficult goals and milestones, he would rarely praise them. He privately confided to those close to him that he would deliberately withhold any praise to his subordinates so that the workers under his leadership would keep working harder in the hope of eventually receiving his ever-elusive approval (see "**Fear Versus Loyalty**").

And it worked, at least in the short term. Fred gained the reputation within the organization's upper leadership as a leader who "could get things done," who could deliver when others couldn't. He was given more responsibility, bigger assignments, and generous awards and promotions. His star was rapidly rising.

But, over time, a funny thing happened. People in the organization slowly became wise to Fred's questionable tactics and his abusive approach in leading his team. Word spread and skilled workers slowly started declining assignments to work on projects under his leadership. Word had gotten out among the working-level employees concerning Fred's true colors, and he quickly became toxic among the rank-and-file workers. People who had no choice but to work for him did so grudgingly, but never expended any extra effort to go above and beyond the call of duty when circumstances suggested that this was needed to get the job done—they reserved that type of extra effort for managers for whom they felt a sense of loyalty and commitment. Instead, those working under Fred would "work to rule," doing no more than they had to for a manager that they neither admired nor respected.

Eventually, Fred's meteoric rise stalled, as did his career. It took quite a while, but Fred's toxic reputation and the growing negative opinion of his abusive leadership practices eventually caught up with him. Negative whisperings about Fred's questionable leadership style made its way up to the upper echelon of the organization, and the senior leadership team there took note … and took action. Last I heard, Fred was shuffled off into an inconsequential role somewhere buried in the organization. His name became a common buzzword within the organization for the type of toxic manager that no one would ever voluntarily choose to work for.

This may seem like an isolated incident, but I have seen versions of this story play out repeatedly over my almost 40-year career. There are a lot of "Freds" out there, all pursuing career advancement and willing to make compromises to attain it. The names and projects may change but the results are typically the same. Promising and ambitious workers buy into the falsehood that, in order to get ahead, one has to compromise ethics and engage in cutthroat and dishonorable practices in order to advance in the workplace. In almost every instance I know of, eventually people become wise to the true colors of these rapid climbers. When this occurs, they become victims of their own compromises and their resultant ill-gotten reputations. This type of approach is, at its core, a self-centered agenda focused on the advancement of one individual over the overall good of the rest of the team or organization. It undermines team dynamics and team culture and ultimately serves as a destabilizing force on the team that they lead.

Fortunately, not everyone agrees with the conclusions that this type of poor behavior sets you on the path to success. Recently, the *Wall Street Journal* weighed in on this with an essay entitled, "You Don't Have to Be a Jerk to Succeed," stating "research suggests that, in most contexts, being disagreeable does not help you to get ahead—and may even be a serious disadvantage."[*]

The reality is that people eventually figure out who the "Freds" of the world are, though it just might take a little while. And, if you find yourself in an organization where "Fred-like" behavior is tolerated (or even encouraged), perhaps it's time for you to start looking for a new place to work that doesn't tolerate this type of behavior.

While this "nice guys finish last" falsehood seems to have remarkable staying power as a guiding principle in the workplace, many have discovered that the *opposite* principle is actually true. Just as the workplace is full of "Freds" and the dubious compromises they make in order to get ahead, there are many examples of managers and supervisors who we'll call the "anti-Freds." These leaders take the opposite approach and have an overwhelmingly positive effect on the project teams that they lead. Through my long career working on numerous spaceflight projects at NASA and with our industry partners, I have witnessed remarkable examples of truly inspirational and sacrificial leadership, individuals who inspire loyalty from those who labor under their leadership. Time and time again, I have seen the game-changing value of such leaders in guiding their teams through difficult and seemingly insurmountable obstacles in order to achieve mission success. Instead of focusing on themselves and their own advancement, these "anti-Freds" put the good of the project first. They also work hard to support the career development and advancement of those who work for them.

---

[*]Y. Mounk. February 1, 2024. "You Don't Have to Be a Jerk to Succeed," *The Wall Street Journal*, www.wsj.com/lifestyle/workplace/you-dont-have-to-be-a-jerk-to-succeed-bfb95774?mod=hp_lead_pos8.

It's no wonder that these types of managers and leaders are regularly promoted into positions of greater responsibility and influence due to their remarkable leadership skills and the positive way they treat those working underneath them.

To be sure, it is a great deal more difficult to be an effective and inspirational leader than a self-centered leader who manipulates others for their own selfish gain. But this more positive approach does provide a more lasting and effective path to rewards and promotion, with none of the pitfalls and traps that selfish leaders eventually face.

****

The popular falsehood that "nice guys finish last" is only one of the many untruths that are readily promulgated (and accepted) in the workplace. I have found, over my career, that the workplace is filled with a multitude of these rarely challenged and generally accepted principles and "truths" that are actually false. Unfortunately, well-meaning people adopt these lies, myths, and misrepresentations and too often suffer the consequences of the poor advice that they convey.

It is unfortunate that so many of today's workers struggle to find reliable advice in today's workplace. Today's working world can be an extremely difficult environment for the typical employee, leaving many of them in great need for trusted sources of practical help on how to navigate the challenges they face.

If you disagree with this statement, just think about what your friends and co-workers talk about when they get together after a long day at work. Start a conversation about work and, before you know it, the conversation will invariably head down the path of the latest challenges and complaints about the job. Virtually everyone has a story about an impossible boss, a difficult co-worker, a challenging deadline, a toxic work environment, a lack of resources, an annoying new policy—the list goes on and on. Even people who *like* their work will grudgingly acknowledge that the workplace can be a difficult place. Studies have shown that while many workers are fairly satisfied with their jobs, this doesn't mean that they don't feel that their workplaces aren't stressful or challenging or include some major factors that they wish were different.

In fact, the rare employee seems to be the one who simply loves their job and has no major complaints. The average worker is in serious need of reliable and effective advice on how to navigate today's workplace challenges. They desperately need help sorting through the lies and half-truths in order to find good, sound, truthful advice to guide them through the difficulties that they face.

My own workplace experiences demonstrated the need to debunk many of the lies and half-truths prevalent in today's workplace. Over the course of my lengthy career, I worked for NASA at Goddard Space Flight Center as part of large multidisciplinary technical teams developing advanced satellite systems, eventually leading large teams in the development of billion-dollar NASA spaceflight missions. During my early years in the workplace, I rarely challenged many of the "truths" of the workplace that are generally accepted as fact—I just assumed that they were true. Over time, however, I began to notice that many of these readily accepted "truths" are actually not true at all. Many are either patently false or are misrepresentations and misunderstandings of how things should function in the workplace. Once they are repeated enough times without being challenged, these falsehoods begin to be accepted by most people as facts.[†] You've probably heard these falsehoods many times yourself and, as a result, likely believe that they're actually true. But they're not.

While many of these so-called truths are actually false, I've also learned over the years that there are a separate set of valuable principles that, if followed, will allow individuals to be substantially more successful in the workplace and in their dealings with others around them.

As a result of a long and successful career leading large teams at NASA, I learned the hard way about how to navigate the complex and challenging environment typified in the modern workplace. As I worked to pass along these hard-won lessons-learned and assist others in navigating workplace survival, I became increasingly disheartened

---

[†] E. Dreyfuss, February 11, 2017, "Want to Make a Lie Seem True? Say It Again. And Again. And Again," Wired.com, www.wired.com/2017/02/dont-believe-lies-just-people-repeat/.

with the lies and misperceptions regularly presented as truth in the workplace. Frustrated with the constant effort required to continually correct workplace falsehoods and prevent them from being accepted by others, I became determined to do something about it. And thus, this book was born.

This book leverages my years of practical, hands-on experience to clearly identify many of the mistruths prevalent in today's workforce. The goal of the following pages is to expose those falsehoods and instead offer proven principles that will assist workers in navigating today's complex and challenging workplace environment. We will highlight, examine, dissect, and address many of the false assumptions that proliferate in the workplace and are readily accepted as unquestioned facts. Just as these lies, half-truths, and misperceptions can cause havoc and disruption in the workplace, there are also time-tested principles that can ease and address workplace challenges and increase harmony and teamwork within the workplace. In the following pages, we will identify and walk through many of those principles. We'll endeavor to not only identify and expose the commonly accepted lies that can lead well-meaning people astray, but also identify the timeless principles that can set you up for workplace success and advancement. While adopting these principles will not serve as a "quick fix" for rapid advancement, following them will allow individuals to establish a firm foundation and a solid reputation on which to build their career. This is true regardless of whether you're in a technical field like I was at NASA or a completely different type of job environment. The lessons and principles described in this book are universal and apply well beyond NASA. In fact, they are applicable to almost *every* workplace environment. These essential principles address how teams are organized and communicate, what teams value, and how they conduct their day-to-day work, and they are designed to help workers better understand and navigate the complexities of workplace relationships between co-workers and across the various layers of an organization. As a result, the principles in this book are applicable to virtually any reader independent of the type of industry or organization in which they are employed.

Each chapter will identify common workplace lies and, alternatively, highlight key principles vital for workplace success. Through presenting these time-tested principles, we'll be providing the reader with examples of practical guidelines and practices that can set them up for workplace success and advancement. All of these examples are drawn from actual workplace experiences. These examples are combined with practical stories and personal anecdotes from the workplace trenches to further illustrate the principles and why they should be followed. Since no principles stand alone, in many cases there will be cross references to other chapters with corollary principles related to the point that is being covered.

The end goal of providing these principles is to share a career of "lessons-learned" to willing listeners to help them successfully navigate through the challenges of the workplace. You will obtain the benefits of a lifetime of workplace experiences without having had to experience the "school of hard knocks" yourself. As I often shared when I taught classes to younger rising engineers, "There are an infinite number of mistakes that you can make in the workplace. You're welcome to make each and every one of these mistakes yourselves. Or, you can listen to the lessons-learned from others and reduce the number of mistakes you make by a few thousand. The choice is yours." The information provided in the book is given with the hope that it will provide the readers a helpful "leg up" and allow them to avoid some of the mistakes they might otherwise make on their own.

With this in mind, hold on tight as we examine the lies, half-truths, and misperceptions readily presented as truth in the workplace, countering them with actual truth and guiding principles intended to help you navigate the complexities of the workplace environment.

CHAPTER 2

Technical Versus Non-Technical Challenges

With the exception of the summers during my college years when I worked as a lifeguard to pay my way through engineering school, I have worked my entire career in highly technical engineering positions. The vast majority of my career has been spent at NASA, which specializes in cutting edge, one-of-a-kind spaceflight missions designed to enable unprecedented scientific discoveries.

Throughout my career, I was told, time and time again, that the biggest issues that most organizations like mine face are dominated by complex technical challenges. In order to address these challenges, the most important skills needed from prospective employees are highly technical. As a result, employers sought out workers with these advanced technical skills and experience, with little regard for any other defining qualifications.

To most people, this assessment sounds accurate and few would disagree with these conclusions. The only problem is that this commonly held belief is actually incorrect.

In reality, as I progressed through my NASA career, I was surprised to discover that the biggest and most predictable challenges that teams face (even technical teams) are typically non-technical in nature. These challenges require employees to utilize a wide variety of non-technical skills in order to successfully navigate them. In fact, even at NASA, many of the technical issues that programs face often have their roots in distinctly non-technical origins. Teams that possess significant technical skills but struggle with non-technical interactions will be ill-equipped for the inevitable challenges that occur daily in the workplace.

When we talk about "technical" challenges, we're talking about those core activities essential to an organization and its unique mission. For

NASA and other similar workplaces, we typically refer to engineering- and science-related activities and the unique challenges they present. For other workplaces, their "technical" activities (and their "technical" challenges) may be different, but represent core activities essential to their type of business. They may refer to financial management for a business workplace, law and jurisprudence for a legal firm, construction for a building and development company, and so on, all describing essential skills (and related challenges) associated with their specific workplace mission. No matter what the type of work being done, every workplace has their share of "technical" challenges unique to their specific business activities.

To be sure, many workplaces (especially NASA!) are replete with complex technical challenges that can be overwhelming and difficult to solve. I've certainly run into my share of seemingly insurmountable technical problems on the NASA missions I've worked on. Although these types of problems may require substantial resources, extraordinary creativity, and significant technical acumen to solve them, most organizations are often well trained and equipped to identify and deal with their unique types of technical challenges. I've seen (and been part of) many instances where organizations rally together and assemble technical "tiger teams" and mini "Manhattan projects" to successfully attack and overcome particularly onerous technical challenges.

However, many organizations are often woefully ill-equipped to handle the non-technical challenges that they face. By non-technical challenges, I am referring to the "people-type" issues that invariably crop up in any large, diverse, multidisciplinary team that needs to work together to achieve a goal. People are complicated, and the interactions between different types of people are invariably complicated as well, often resulting in disconnects and issues. These non-technical "people-type" issues can manifest themselves through poor communication, turf battles, conflicting agendas, technical disconnects, conflicting cultures, lack of team cohesion, poor leadership, and conflicting personalities, to name a few. Anyone who has worked in a team environment is familiar with these problems and knows that they exist, to some degree, in *every* team. Non-technical "people-type" issues like these complicate communication and the open exchange of information, making the technical challenges even more difficult. Most technical training for a specific business type focuses exclusively on addressing technical issues unique to that workplace and their mission, often with very little focus on helping individuals understand and learn to deal with the non-technical "people-type" minefields that are part of every project (see **"The Need for 'Soft Skills' in a 'Hard Skill' World"**). Like technical issues, non-technical "people-type" issues also have the potential to slow or derail progress. In many cases, as we will see in the subsequent pages of this book, non-technical issues often eventually manifest themselves in actual technical problems and even mission-related failures.

As I've mentioned, every NASA mission I worked on faced its share of serious and seemingly insurmountable technical and design issues. However, with the knowledge that technical challenges are inevitable on NASA missions, NASA has developed over many years a clear and detailed process for addressing technical issues that arise, and our teams were fully trained in how to follow these processes. Not only were our engineers trained and experienced in their specific areas of expertise, but NASA also had a detailed and documented process to identify, diagnose, track, and resolve hardware and software issues as they arose. We had databases that tracked the status of open issues and their path to resolution. There was an entire infrastructure set up to identify and close technical issues and ensure that they did not impact our spacecraft development. Our mission team was required to report on technical issues and their status every month in our regular status meetings and provide detailed summaries at every major project review. Like every other NASA project, we were trained and well-equipped to identify and deal with these types of issues and had clear and established processes to track, address, and close them.

But there was *nothing* like this type of process for addressing the non-technical "people-type" issues. These types of issues, due to their complicated nature, are typically much harder to identify and often much more difficult to understand and address. Most non-technical "people-type" issues tended to linger and often stayed below the radar. If these types of "people-type" issues were brought to light, they were in quietly, behind closed doors, if they were dealt with at all. worse, in many cases it was these lingering "people-type" issues that eventually grew into other issues on the mission and often helped aggravate or even create technical issues.

When I first discovered the prevalence of "non-technical" issues in technical workplaces, I assumed that I must have been mistaken. Fortunately, NASA has a large community of experienced engineers and other technical personnel that I could tap for feedback. To my surprise, as I shared my observations within the community, everyone I spoke to strongly agreed with my conclusions. Almost to a person, they agreed that, while every mission clearly faces technical challenges, the biggest and most repeated challenges that NASA missions face tend to be non-technical "people-type" issues. Additionally, these problems tend to repeat themselves on each subsequent mission. *While we couldn't always predict the specific technical challenges we would face from mission to mission, we could predict with astonishing accuracy the same "non-technical" issues that would crop up on virtually every mission.* As one senior technical lead wryly remarked, "Most of our biggest problems tend to be primarily 'carbon-based.'"

If technical teams and workplace organizations focus primarily on technical challenges, they will miss dealing with the non-technical challenges that plague most workplaces, silently undermining technical progress, productivity, and team cohesion. A well-run organization will be aware of the existence and impact of non-technical challenges, even in technical fields, and put in place measures to train their employees to understand and navigate them.

Guiding Principle: Most organizations are typically well prepared to address technical challenges that arise in their particular workplace. However, many are less aware and ill-equipped to deal with the non-technical "people-type" challenges they face, which may threaten to undermine projects and impact workplace cohesion. Prepared organizations will work to understand and address non-technical minefields.

CHAPTER 3

The Need for "Soft Skills" in a "Hard Skill" World

When I was in college, virtually all of my coursework focused on the technical skills that I needed to learn in order to get a job as an engineer. Later, after I started working as an engineer and went back to school to get my master's degree, all of my courses were again completely technically oriented. It never even crossed my mind to take any courses that were other than technically focused in nature, as I believed that these were exclusively the skills I would need in the workplace. I would learn later that this was certainly *not* the case.

When employers hire personnel, their focus is almost exclusively on discovering the key technical skills that prospective employees possess. By technical skills, we are speaking of the core professional skills required by a specific job description. These could be engineering or computer skills, accounting or bookkeeping skills, or other assorted professional skills essential to do a required job for a particular workplace. Most hiring organizations believe that excellent professional technical skills are the key measure of an employee's potential effectiveness in the workplace. This belief appears to be backed up by the hiring practices of most organizations, which focus almost exclusively on the "hard skills" and technical proficiencies that a particular job requires.

Sadly, this is yet another false assumption that is often passed down through the workplace, often with disastrous workplace results. It's not that technical skills aren't important—they certainly are. Unfortunately, many employers often miss the critical importance of non-technical "people-type" skills in the workplace.

In my early days at NASA, I wholeheartedly believed in the importance of technical excellence above all else. Nothing could convince me otherwise. I firmly believed that staffing projects with technical experts, not only in the leadership roles but also in the engineering teams, was all that was necessary to successfully execute a NASA mission. To my surprise, my experiences on NASA projects clearly demonstrated that this is *not* correct. While technical skill is absolutely essential, it is not sufficient on its own to get the job done properly and achieve mission success. Even in a technical world like NASA, "soft skills" are absolutely necessary to achieve successful workplace results. We saw this in the last chapter (see **"Technical Versus Non-Technical Challenges"**), where we identified that some of the most challenging problems even in technical workplaces were distinctly non-technical in nature. It would make sense, then, that the employees in these workplaces would require a supplemental set of skills to effectively deal with these non-technical challenges.

When we are talking about technical skills, we are typically referring to what is known as "hard skills." Hard skills are specific measurable competencies, knowledge, and abilities that are required to perform a specific task or role. These types of skills are typically acquired through a series of concrete steps via formal education and training programs, including college, apprenticeships, short-term training classes, online courses, and certification programs, as well as on-the-job training. They are often technically oriented, are usually documented and demonstrated by degrees and certificates, and can be readily assessed through external evaluation or demonstration.

Soft skills, on the other hand, are personality traits, social skills, and competencies used to conduct effective interpersonal activities with others. Sometimes, these are also called "people skills" because they directly affect an individual's ability to interact and work alongside others in complex social and workplace situations. Soft skills are often linked to an individual's personality, but they can be taught and developed over time through training and practice. Unfortunately, there are very few formal training courses where "soft skills" are taught. The focus of most classroom instruction and training courses is often exclusively devoted to passing on "hard skills." Unlike hard skills, the acquisition of soft skills is difficult to measure and often subjective, making training and development of these skills more difficult than hard skills. Hard skills can be demonstrated through degrees, certifications, and testing, while soft skills are best demonstrated over time in real-life situations, making them difficult to assess and document.

Recognizing the need for these skills in the workplace, LinkedIn, the online professional networking site, rated the five top "soft skills" that were most needed in the workplace:[*]

- Creativity
- Persuasion
- Collaboration
- Adaptability
- Emotional Intelligence

Looking at this list, it is clear that individuals working as part of a multidisciplinary technical team need not only technical (or "hard") skills, but also a healthy dose of "soft skills." A team that practices these types of soft skills will likely be better equipped to overcome many of the interpersonal challenges that inevitably crop up in working within a large multidisciplinary team, even one devoted to a technical task. After all, despite the technical focus of the job, people are still involved, resulting in "people-type" issues. Conversely, a team that lacks the soft skills listed earlier will likely struggle significantly in working together as a cohesive team, perhaps more so in a technically oriented endeavor.

Despite the need for people with "soft skills" in technical teams, employers and those building technical teams tend to hire technical workers primarily based on their "hard skills." The overriding goal in most hiring is to ensure that the candidate's technical background and proficiency are sufficient to complete an assigned task. Employers and team leaders typically don't spend nearly enough effort in understanding a candidate's "soft skills." Assessing a candidate's soft skills is particularly hard to do in a job interview. Any assessment in this area is often limited to how the candidate presents themselves in an hour-long interview and whether the interviewer gets a "good feeling" about the

---

[*]A. Van Nuys, December 28, 2019, "New LinkedIn Research: Upskill Your Employees With the Skills Companies Need Most in 2020," LinkedIn, www.linkedin.com/business/learning/blog/learning-and-development/most-in-demand-skills-2020.

candidate. Sometimes, an interviewer will check references or previous job experience to determine the candidate's history of working alongside others. However, these types of inquiries are typically not very revealing unless the feedback received is extremely positive or negative. As previously mentioned, technical skills can be readily evaluated through degrees and evaluation even in an interview, while soft skills typically only reveal themselves over time in real-life situations. Yet, an individual with poor "soft skills," even though a qualified technical expert in a given area, can render themselves ineffective and even disrupt an entire team.

The teaming environment present in almost every workplace is the driving factor in the need for soft skills. A single person working alone at a computer, workstation, or lab bench likely doesn't have a driving need to acquire and demonstrate soft skills. The absence of these skills will likely have minimal impact, since an individual in this type of role has limited interaction or coordination with others. However, as individuals begin interacting more and more with others, "people-type" issues threaten to arise. As these types of inter-team interactions grow, the importance of "soft skills" to enhance team cohesion and avoid conflicts become more and more important. A healthy team with good "soft skills" can more readily overcome "people-type" non-technical issues and devote more energy and focus on addressing actual technical issues and can do so in a synergistic way.

My observations over my almost 40-year engineering career have revealed a surprising truth—the most effective and sought-after engineers are *not* those who are technical experts. Instead, the ones regularly in demand are often the less-skilled engineers who excel in communication skills, team dynamics, working with others, and the numerous other soft skills that actually make one successful in the workplace. These are the engineers that are regularly sought after to lead multidisciplinary teams and find themselves drafted for bigger and better projects. People who have the interpersonal skills to effectively deal with co-workers and clients at work will *always* do better than their counterparts in dealing with workplace challenges. Conversely, people who do not have these important skill sets will always be less successful.

Unsurprisingly, these skills are needed not just in the NASA technical environment, but also in other technical and non-technical workplaces. In every organization, "people-type" issues are a major cause of workplace disruptions, lost productivity, and staffing issues, and can even result in lawsuits and other unfortunate legal proceedings. Even though I received significant training and tools designed to assist me in resolving technical issues, I was often woefully unprepared for the continual onslaught of non-technical "people-type" issues I would face and received little to no training on dealing with non-technical "people-type" problems that would regularly arise. This seems to be a common theme in most organizations. Most workplaces provide little focused training to assist people in navigating these "people-type" issues. Most employees are left to their own devices to develop these much-needed soft skills, typically resorting to individual personal initiative and learning through "the school of hard knocks," hoping to gain these skills through work and life experiences. Such an ad hoc approach is hardly an optimum way of addressing this type of challenging problem. If NASA attacked our engineering technical problems in the same fashion, we would have many, many more mission failures.

Soft skills are absolutely vital for success in the workplace, even in highly technical careers. Anyone who seeks to be successful in the workplace, whether it is a technical or non-technical organization, will require significant "soft skills" to navigate the people-type issues that they will inevitably encounter. Those who learn to grow and excel in these types of soft skills will certainly see more success and workplace effectiveness than those who lack them, and they will likely achieve greater career advancement.

Guiding Principle: "Soft skills" are an absolute necessity in every workplace, even in a "hard skill" technically oriented environment. Employees who possess substantial soft skills will be better equipped than their peers to navigate the complex interpersonal issues inherent in every workplace organization and will be more likely to achieve successful workplace results.

CHAPTER 4

Building Your Community

I was at the retirement party for Joe, a senior NASA engineer (and good friend) who had finally decided to retire from NASA and start the next stage of his life. The room was filled with other well-respected engineers and managers, a testament to this man's influence and impact during his NASA career.

One after another, people stood up to share humorous and moving stories about Joe, the challenges that they had faced together, how much they enjoyed working with him, and how much he would be missed.

Finally, Joe took the microphone. Always a humble and generous man, he thanked everyone for what he felt was overstated praise. I don't remember much of what he shared, but there is one thing he said that stood out.

Joe held up the Goddard Space Flight Center phone book (back when we still actually used a real paper phone book!) and said, "Of all the tools I used in my years at NASA, this was the most valuable one I had. The people who I worked with were the key to any success I had. I could pick up the phone whenever I got stuck, and I could always find someone in my community of coworkers who could help me out of whatever challenge I was facing."

There is a fundamental truth in what Joe shared that day that many people miss. The 17th-century English author John Donne is famous for saying "No man is an island," meaning that no one is self-sufficient and that everyone relies on others. I have absolutely found this to be true. No person knows everything, and we all need help. We are only as strong as the community of people we build around us. This is particularly true at NASA and in the spaceflight business. It is likely true in your workplace as well.

Too often, there may be subtle pressure in the workplace not to seek out others for assistance or help when we need it. Perhaps there's the fear that we may appear to be inadequate or that we don't have all the answers. This is a dangerous way of thinking and needs to be exposed for the fallacy that it is. The reality is that no one person has all the answers, and the ability to network and share information with others should be seen as a great strength, not a sign of weakness. Like my friend Joe, building a community of trusted advisors and experts around us makes us stronger, not weaker.

There is a key characteristic I have observed that seems to be common among successful senior technical leaders. Without fail, all of them have, over the years, built a community of experienced and trusted advisors and technical experts that they have worked with over the course of their careers. Rather than simply move on after a given job is over and let these contacts go, they have preserved them as valued contacts that they regularly go to when they need assistance with challenging problems. This assistance may be purely technical, or it may be to tap the experiences and advice of trusted contacts when tackling tough non-technical issues. It takes years to develop a deep bench of these contacts, but they are invaluable in navigating the challenges that constantly arise in the workplace.

When I started my NASA career, I was inexperienced and unfamiliar with the culture at Goddard, often finding myself stuck and needing help. Over the course of many years, I slowly discovered who to go to for help with various technical issues when I needed assistance. It became clear to me that I did not possess sufficient technical expertise to solve most problems by myself, and Goddard was filled with people with greater technical abilities than my own. Over the years and over many missions, I slowly developed a network of "go to" contacts to visit when I needed help or advice (which was often).

Through this process, I learned to surround myself with people who were smarter and more talented than I was. Some people are wary of such an approach, afraid that they will be overshadowed by people who appear to be more gifted than they are. Ironically, I found just the opposite to be true. I not only benefited personally by seeking out talented people to assist me in solving tough problems, but received positive feedback from my management for my ability to surround myself with skilled and talented workers. A co-worker even remarked to me once, "Management was smart to give you this job, because you always do a great job of surrounding yourself with the best people."

The missions at NASA present many difficult challenges, both technical and non-technical. When we surround ourselves with skilled technical experts, we are always stronger than when we go about it on our own. Not only do we learn from these people in solving technical challenges, but these collaborations help us to grow in our character and non-technical skills. We also build a community of valued contacts who become our "go to" bench of advisors for any future instances when we may need them again.

The process of building this community can take many forms. There are people I go to time and time again for assistance, and I often joke that the carpet is worn out between my office and theirs from the frequent foot traffic. It is obvious that I consider them to be trusted co-workers and valued sources of input. Sometimes, however, I may choose to be very direct in how I communicate my appreciation, wanting there to be no mistake that I appreciated the assistance I received. When there is an individual who has worked for me on a project or task and has done an excellent job and supported me well, I will go out of my way to thank and appreciate them, telling them "You're part of my work community now. Feel free to reach out to me anytime you need help or assistance." All of us appreciate hearing when our contributions have made a difference and this is an excellent way to build goodwill and add to your list of helpful contacts for the future.

Who do you surround yourself with? Do they make you better? Do they challenge you? Do they help you solve problems at work? The type of people you choose to surround yourself with says a great deal about who you are. Your chosen community has great potential to challenge and mold you into a better worker and a better person. Years ago, I read a Japanese proverb that stuck with me and I think of often: "When the character of a man is not clear to you, look at his friends," meaning that an individual can be best understood by examining the company that they voluntarily choose to associate with. The *Book of Proverbs* states the truth of the influential power of our chosen community much more succinctly: "He who walks with wise men will become wise." Surrounding yourself with a wise, experienced, and helpful community of trusted advisors and technical experts will significantly help with navigating challenges that arise in the workplace.

Guiding Principle: Be intentional to build a community of people who can help you and make you better. Wise leaders take the time to build a bench of experienced contacts who they can go to for assistance with the inevitable technical and non-technical challenges they face in the workplace.

CHAPTER 5

A Failure to Communicate

There is a commonly held belief, especially in technically oriented fields, that communication skills are not essential to job performance. Technical experts don't need to be good communicators, the thinking goes, as long as they are technically excellent in their fields of expertise. Any weaknesses in communication skills can be more than made up with technical excellence.

Unfortunately, this too is a widely believed falsehood that needs to be debunked.

I recall a conversation I had once with NASA's Chief Engineer, who shared with me that virtually every NASA failure could be attributed to a breakdown or failure in communication. I was stunned. Here was the top technical leader at NASA, responsible for ensuring the technical readiness and execution of NASA missions, stating that the chief cause of NASA failures was ... a failure to communicate properly? In disbelief, I set off on my own to verify this ... and discovered that he was correct. Virtually every NASA failure I examined had a fundamental root cause that could be attributed to a breakdown in communication, eventually leading to a larger problem or failure.

I can understand how technically-oriented individuals might be tempted to lean hard into the idea that communication skills are not that essential. In my experience, engineers and technical experts are often, by nature, not the best communicators and often are not well-trained in dealing with interpersonal matters and conflicts. There are exceptions, of course, but my experience has shown me that the skills and expertise of highly technical people typically lie elsewhere. As a result, communication is an area they would prefer to minimize. However, communication lapses can be a major cause of issues, even in a technical environment.

I recall my first NASA mission when I had been recently assigned as the Product Development Lead responsible for leading a team in the development of a flight avionics unit for an advanced NASA spacecraft. Anxious not to make a mistake on my first major assignment, I made sure our team met with all the key spacecraft subsystems early in the design process, working out the details of the interfaces between our avionics unit and the rest of the spacecraft. My goal was to ensure that all the engineers were on the same page and there were no errors or misunderstandings. It was a time-consuming process, but one I felt was absolutely necessary to ensure that we would not run into a problem later that would impact design, schedule, and cost.

After our team had developed a working breadboard of our design, the most experienced person on our young team (the only one who had previously worked on a flight mission) suggested we conduct an early interface test with the subsystem team down the hall. The plan was simple and straightforward—bring both teams' breadboards into the lab, hook them together for a test run, and verify that they worked according to design. Most of the team felt that this test was unneeded and a waste of precious time, especially considering our busy schedule, but the engineer pressed for the test and we ultimately agreed. We coordinated with the other team, set up the lab, and ran the test, expecting everything to run smoothly on this test that we really didn't need.

Unexpectedly, the test failed.

It turns out that, despite all of our communication on the interface details, we had made some assumptions that led to miscommunication errors. These miscommunications were later incorporated into the design, causing the interface to be inoperable. I'm sorry to say, finger-pointing ensued. Eventually, both of our teams realized that we had a choice—continue to blame the other side for the error and further delay the schedule or adopt a humbler attitude and focus our efforts on fixing the problem. With this in mind, we shook off our failure and quickly solved the interface issue. Fortunately, thanks to the foresight of the engineer on our team who pushed for the early test, the impact of the redesign was limited to our bruised egos, and we learned a valuable lesson on the importance of communication.

This example stuck with me throughout my career, serving as a reminder that communication lapses and missteps can occur even when teams are aggressively working to make sure that clear and open communication lines are in place. That is why intentional, clear, and open communication is paramount. This is true not only for teams working together on complex NASA missions, but in any teaming organization. Fortunately, in my example, our issues were caught and corrected early with little impact. Sadly, this is not always the case. NASA has a number of examples where communication issues slipped through undetected, resulting in the degradation or loss of high-profile missions.

The more differences and complexities there are within a team, the greater the potential for miscommunication to occur and the greater the need for an intentional focus on improving communication. The introduction of a "remote workplace" environment (where co-workers don't have regular face-to-face contact) only exacerbates this challenge. In our case, despite being on the same project team, in the same organization, on the same hallway, and having early interface meetings, a communication error still occurred and led to an interface error. In cases where the differences are even greater—different organizations, geographic separation, cultural differences, and so on—the chances for miscommunication can increase dramatically. For example, some of my co-workers worked on joint missions between NASA and the Japan Aerospace Exploration Agency and would share with me the significant communication challenges that they regularly faced. In their case, they faced major geographical differences, time zone differences, language differences, and significant cultural differences that directly impacted every aspect of communication. The teams on both sides had to be very intentional to ensure that communication was clear and understood by everyone. After every major meeting and decision, they would follow up later to ensure that there were no miscommunications or misunderstandings.

In addition to inadvertent communication issues, on every project there are the inevitable instances of people who choose, for whatever reason, not to communicate openly with their counterparts. As a result, communication lines atrophy, slowing or stopping the transmission of critical information and risking technical disconnects. This can be a more difficult problem to address, with underlying issues that may need to be dealt with (see **"Are You Better Off With Them or Without Them?"**).

While systems engineering relies heavily on technical expertise, it is largely a *communication activity*. This can be a significant challenge, especially since most engineers are not necessarily natural communicators. In addition, engineers tend to love their data and often feel that "more is better" when it comes to providing engineering data and analysis to their audience. This trait can lead to overloading the recipient and inadvertently obscuring the important core message with too much information. These factors increase the challenges of effectively communicating with a diverse audience, especially where some of the participants may not be technically oriented or may come from different backgrounds. Coming up with strategies for effective communication inside and outside the team is one of the key responsibilities of the lead systems engineer and any leader of a multidisciplinary team.

The number one thing an effective leader can do to set their team up for success is to create an environment characterized by clear, open, honest, and effective communication. This positions the team to effectively assess and respond to whatever challenges come their way. No organization can succeed without effective communication. An organization where this is missing may be able to limp along for a time, but ultimately will start to fall apart from within due to miscommunication, conflicts, and various assorted other issues that will prevent them from succeeding. When people feel that they cannot speak up honestly or are hindered from open communication, the organization is hampered from receiving honest and helpful feedback that drives improvement and provides corrective changes (see **"No Stupid Questions Allowed"**). With this in mind, wise and proactive leaders will do everything in their power to ensure open and honest communication throughout the organization, providing numerous opportunities for this at every level.

Creating a culture within an organization that encourages open communication is essential to its continued success. Sometimes all it takes is to remind the team members of the need to communicate and the potential consequences of faulty communication. In many cases, however, more systemic and intentional efforts may be necessary. These efforts may include aggressively promoting positive and open communication by a variety of means—whether by face-to-face meetings, walking around and touching base with team members, or doing whatever it takes to foster regular, open communication and build positive working relationships. Recognizing the importance of clear and open communication in solving and preventing problems, wise team leaders institute regular, planned team meetings. While many are tempted to view such meetings as a waste of valuable time, the converse is often true. I always saw these team meetings as a valuable connection time with my entire team. Not only do these meetings serve as an opportunity to discuss and solve technical issues, but they also provide the chance to "take the temperature" of the team, work through disagreements and differences, and build relationships and trust. They also create valuable opportunities to work with the team to honestly self-assess and discuss the culture of the team (see **"Creating a Team Culture"**) and strategize areas of improvement. Outside the meetings, I would make a point to follow up with team members to make sure there were no hidden issues or concerns that were not getting adequate exposure in our group meetings. These simple actions are not remotely groundbreaking, which is exactly the point: Communication does not need to be elaborate or innovative, it just needs to happen.

Guiding Principle: Good communication is essential for teams to be successful, and communication breakdowns are a primary cause of technical and non-technical workplace issues. Good leaders make clear, open, honest, and frequent communication a top (if not *the* top) priority and lead by example in instilling this into the team culture.

CHAPTER 6

The Value of a Mentor

Finding a mentor is, from a career growth perspective, really not that important. You can just as easily learn things on your own. In fact, most mentoring programs appear to be dreamed up by human resource departments and are typically "check-the-box" activities with no real value to the participants or to their career development.

Or so I thought, early in my career. Most of my experiences with mentoring assignments were lackluster at best. Typically, this process was part of a "new employee" program, something mandated by the organization that, frankly, wasn't very helpful or effective. My mentors weren't very inspiring and, as a result, I wasn't very inspired. I certainly didn't feel like I was getting much out of these assigned mentoring exchanges and the whole process seemed to be a waste of my valuable time.

This was my perspective on mentoring for a long time. That is, until I met Mike.

Ironically, when I first met Mike, I immediately decided that I didn't like him at all. Little did I know that he would become the single most influential figure across my entire NASA career.

We first met at an early design peer review, where a member of my team was presenting an initial design concept that we had worked hard on and of which I was especially proud. We had done our homework and had come up with what we thought was a clever design approach. As a result, I was confident that the review would go well.

Not long into the review, a man in the audience politely raised his hand and started asking some questions about our design. I didn't know him and guessed he had been invited by the project management team.

After asking a few questions, this man (who shared that his name was Mike) walked over to the whiteboard and, as he spoke, quickly sketched out an alternative design concept to ours. As he was doing so, he encouraged us to consider it and suggested this alternate approach would make our design simpler and more reliable.

I was caught completely by surprise at how quickly our well-thought-out design (from my perspective) fell apart under Mike's quick evaluation. More than that, I was mad. First, this guy crashed our well-planned peer review and questioned our design with some seat-of-the-pants alternative concept. Second (and even more offensive), as he scribbled on the whiteboard, I could quickly see that his scribbled design was far superior to our carefully constructed (yet obviously inferior) approach.

I realized—at that moment—that I had a choice to make. Either I could choose to be upset that this guy had thrown a monkey wrench into our review, *or* I could swallow my pride, go up to this fellow, talk to him, and pick his brain for ideas. It was obvious that he knew what he was talking about, and that he was smarter and more experienced than I (or my team) was. On top of this, the project management team obviously trusted him enough to invite him to the review.

In a decision that I often look back on and pat myself on the back for, I swallowed my pride and went up to talk to this annoying guy who had torpedoed my well-planned review. It was the beginning of a partnership where I benefitted far more than I could have possibly imagined.

It turns out, Mike was not only smarter and more experienced than I imagined, but was a veteran of multiple successful NASA missions and was eager to teach anyone who was willing to learn. On top of this, he was also very humble and an all-around nice guy. He was more than glad to share his expertise and became a huge help to our design team. We became friends and very soon I came to see him as a trusted mentor as well. In fact, Mike has been a trusted mentor and advisor on almost every mission I have worked on. While I have been blessed with many excellent teachers, mentors, and peers, I have learned more about developing and operating spacecraft from Mike than probably most of these people put together. Whenever I get stuck or need either technical help or simply good advice, Mike is the first guy I go to.

Needless to say, my opinion on the value of finding a mentor has dramatically shifted since my initial negative perspective. Since that time, I have found many other people who I consider to be mentors. All of my mentors were men and women who I identified over the course of my career, people who I saw had characteristics that I envied and admired and I thought had something to teach me. As a result, I made a point of seeking them out, asking questions, and trying to soak in as much knowledge and wisdom as I could. I now believe that finding a good mentor is one of the most important things that an individual can do to grow and advance in their career. If you don't think that mentoring is valuable, I daresay that this is probably because you haven't found the right mentor yet.

My role as a NASA systems engineer covered an astonishingly broad area of complicated technical subjects, including mission requirements, design and implementation details, and operations concepts. It is impossible for any one individual to possess sufficient experience or expertise to understand the complete system and its nuances and issues. I suspect this is true of many other technical areas within other workplaces as well. Even the most brilliant and talented individuals will require help to understand and navigate the broad technical areas required in most technically oriented positions. In my experience, one of the most significant things that an engineer or aspiring leader can do to grow and develop in the workplace is to enter into an effective mentoring relationship with a more experienced leader. A mentoring relationship is one where a more experienced person (mentor) takes a less experienced person (mentee) under their wing with the express purpose of transferring their knowledge and experience and offering advice. A key goal in this partnership is to help the mentee progress more quickly in their development than they would have done on their own. In addition to bringing practical experience and knowledge, the mentor often serves as an advisor, coach, and sounding board to the mentee. A wise individual will build an informal bench of these types of more experienced mentors and peers as go-to contacts for dealing with the many technical (and non-technical) issues that will inevitably arise. As my friend Joe shared in a previous chapter (see **"Building Your Community"**), this fellowship of mentors and peers has the potential to become one of the most valuable tools in any leader's toolbox.

Some people tend to get hung up on the term "mentor", which can sound awfully formal and a bit intimidating. In these cases, it might be helpful to reframe this role as more of a coach—someone with more experience than you in an important area who can help you succeed. Such a coach can serve as a guide, helper, and motivator to help you grow and achieve in a manner that you couldn't have done as quickly or perhaps as effectively had you been left to your own devices. Whatever you choose to call this role, having help from an experienced and trusted advisor will always help an individual progress faster than they would have done on their own.

Here are a few helpful tips I have learned over the years on establishing a mentoring relationship:

- **Start early**—We have a saying in our family, "The wrong time to start learning how to swim is when you find yourself drowning." In the same way, it is often a bit late to look for a trusted confidant and technical advisor when you find yourself deep in trouble. It would be far better to have established a mentoring and advising relationship *before* you find yourself in trouble or needing help, as this relationship would already be in place when you needed it. In addition, the earlier in your career you establish this mentoring relationship, the sooner you can benefit from the many advantages it provides.
- **Characteristics of a good mentor**—Obviously, a key attribute in a good mentoring candidate is finding someone who has valuable knowledge and experience worth passing along. However, a good mentor is much more than that. Just because someone is smart and technically astute doesn't necessarily mean that they will be a good mentor—some smart people turn out to be terrible mentors and are simply unsuited for this role. Here are some fundamental characteristics that you should be looking for in a prospective mentor:
  - *Willing*: A good mentor is first and foremost a willing participant, helpful, and glad to train others. Enlisting a mentor who is not wholeheartedly onboard with the idea

of working to teach an aspiring employee is a recipe for disappointment or failure.
    - *Affinity*: The best mentoring relationships are those where there is some rapport between mentor and mentee. Obviously, in a positive mentoring relationship, this rapport will grow over time, but there needs to be some degree of affinity or common ground to start with. This is one of the reasons why successful mentoring relationships often start by first identifying someone more senior on your team or within your organization who you feel that you can relate to in addition to someone you can learn from, then using your observations as a springboard to start initiating a mentoring relationship.
    - *Approachable and safe*: Effective mentoring relationships need to have a degree of honesty and transparency that allows frank and straightforward conversations, where the mentee is free to safely admit what they don't understand or discuss issues that they are currently facing. Again, this openness will develop over time, but the relationship needs to feel "safe" at the beginning in order to create an environment where honest communication can grow.
    - *Available*: It doesn't matter how good the mentor is or how helpful the growing relationship has the potential to be, if the mentor is too busy to meet regularly, then the relationship will never have a chance to grow. Effective relationships are steadily built over time and a mentoring relationship is no different.
- **Assigned or selected**—My own personal view of "assigned" mentors is similar to my view on arranged marriages—I've heard of cases where it works, but I would much rather have a say in choosing my own. This view is based on my own experience with assigned mentors—rarely has it worked out to my satisfaction. However, when I've sought out and developed mentoring contacts over time on my own (usually following the tips I've just listed previously), I've been able to build up a bench

of some amazing working relationships who I have been able to learn valuable lessons from.

Choosing your own mentor may not be practical, however, either because an existing mentoring program is already set up to choose formal mentors or a new employee doesn't yet have the breadth of relationships such that selecting a "good fit" mentor is a practical solution. Even if mentors are assigned, there needs to be some allowance for feedback from the mentee (typically based on the above "Characteristics of a good mentor") to assess whether a mentoring match is a good fit. In addition, there is no rule I know of that states you can only have one mentor—even if your program assigns you a mentor, you can still seek out additional mentors on your own. I have cultivated a number of diverse mentoring relationships that I regularly tap for help and advice depending on the specific need at hand.

- **Approaching a potential mentor**—There are many possible ways to initiate a mentoring relationship. I recommend letting the mentoring relationship develop naturally. If you find that there is someone you regularly go to for advice, who seems to have answers and experience, who is approachable and available, and with whom you feel that there is some shared affinity, you've likely spotted a potential mentor. Start by doing what you're already doing—continue to approach the potential mentor with questions as they come up, seeking their input and advice. If they are a good mentoring fit for you, this regular process of seeking their advice will slowly grow into the relationship you're looking for. If they are not a good fit, you'll likely find out pretty quickly. Finally, there's no rule that you have to formally define your mentoring relationship—sometimes it is fine to just let it grow naturally. In my case, after going to Mike for over 25 years and seeking his input and help, I finally shared with him one day that I had always seen him as a valued mentor. His response was priceless—he looked shocked and caught off guard and didn't know what to say. He had apparently always seen us as a pair of trusted colleagues working together despite his vastly superior knowledge and experience. His honest humility was yet another reason why he was an invaluable mentor.

While we've talked about setting up a mentoring relationship and the characteristics of a good mentor, a vital ingredient we haven't yet broached is *your* ability to learn from your mentor. Oftentimes, like my first meeting with my mentor Mike, it means having a willingness to park your pride and ego at the door and adopting sufficient humility to be able to admit that you have something to learn. Most people who are hungry to learn and grow are willing to do this, but some aren't. This willingness to learn on the part of the mentee is an absolutely essential ingredient that is important to mention.

Finding a good mentor is not a "magic bullet" for success, but it is a really good start. Developing a trusted relationship with a more experienced leader will not only help you grow and develop more quickly than you would without one, but it also provides you with a valuable sounding board and a place for coaching when challenges arise where you may need assistance on how to proceed.

Guiding Principle: Entering into effective mentoring relationships with a more experienced leader is one of the most significant things that an engineer or aspiring technical leader can do to rapidly grow and develop in the workplace. A good mentor will not only provide wise technical advice, but will also serve as an effective advisor, coach, and sounding board in addressing issues as they arise.

CHAPTER 7

What, Me a Mentor?

Rick was one of the best guys on my team, but he had one nagging problem—he kept getting frustrated with the younger, less experienced workers on the team. Whenever one of these younger folks would ask him a question, Rick had trouble containing his obvious annoyance.

It took me a while, but I finally figured out the problem. Rick, despite his years of experience on multiple missions, saw himself as simply an average guy. As a result, he couldn't understand why these younger folks couldn't see for themselves what was so obvious to him. If he could understand things, Rick reasoned, why couldn't they? I reminded him that he was actually one of the most knowledgeable guys on my team, with a tremendous amount of experience to offer these younger workers. In fact, just as Rick's mentors and co-workers had helped build his career, now he needed to do the same for others.

This situation highlights a common falsehood that many experienced workers tell themselves—that they have nothing meaningful to teach and pass on to others, despite their experience. The reality is, many of these individuals actually do have a wealth of knowledge and practical experience that younger employees would greatly benefit from. Many of them would likely make excellent mentors to more junior employees. They may just need some help and encouragement to see themselves and their skills in the proper light to realize their potential benefit to others.

As difficult as it was for Rick to see himself in that light, he finally got it. Although he had a hard time viewing himself as a mentor, with some encouragement he decided to give it a try. He eventually became an excellent mentor once he realized that he actually had something worth passing on, and he became instrumental in training and guiding many younger engineers.

I have found that cases like Rick's are surprisingly common. Most skilled workers who are used to being mentored by others often struggle with the idea that they might have something valuable to pass on and build into the next generation. I suspect that the most common question that prospective new mentors ask themselves is "Do I really have anything worthwhile to teach?" It may also be that an individual is so used to being the "student" that they just can't fathom actually being a "teacher". I wonder if we have made mentoring sound so grandiose or complicated that it scares potential mentors off, making them feel inadequate for such a lofty assignment. I have found that almost everyone has something valuable that they can pass along to others, which is exactly what mentoring is all about. Effective mentoring is really just walking alongside someone on their workplace journey, answering questions as they come up. This may be as simple as just sharing stories about your own journey, what worked for you and what didn't, and how this might be applicable to them.

Some potential mentors, like Rick, set an impossibly high bar for themselves on the amount of knowledge and experience that they need to possess before they could possibly undertake a mentoring assignment. It doesn't help that a mentoring discussion often conjures up images of gray-haired wise men dispensing sage wisdom gathered from the ages. The reality is that helping someone on their workplace journey simply means that you need to have traveled a bit further on your journey than they have, allowing you to give helpful tips and suggestions to those who follow you. In fact, having recent workplace experience similar to what another person may be going through may be more advantageous than experiences that are in your distant past. Instead of your memories being dim, recent experiences would stand out more clearly, with any lessons learned still fresh in your mind. Conversely, if a prospective mentor is planning to be the fount of all knowledge and wisdom and bestow this on their mentee, they're probably not the right person for the job. Instead of knowledge transfer being the primary mentoring function, I have found that a great deal of mentoring is listening, seeking to understand, and pointing people in the right direction. Never underestimate the value an individual feels in knowing that they have someone firmly in their corner who is listening to and rooting for them. A good mentor provides assurance to their mentee that they have a trusted and confidential sounding board to go to, someone who will act on their behalf or serve as an advocate if needed. These non-technical assurances are just as important aspects of mentoring as simply passing on knowledge and experience.

In a previous section, we covered the qualities to look for in a mentor (see **"The Value of a Mentor"**), so we won't cover them again here. One important caveat to any prospective mentoring assignment is to first make absolutely sure that the person you are offering to mentor actually *wants* to be mentored and sees value in this activity. I have learned to always ask this question, as this is a fundamental ingredient in any successful mentoring relationship. Curiously, whenever I ask the individuals I have been assigned to if they actually *want* a mentor, the answer always seems to be an unequivocal "Yes", yet I have also found that many times this is not the case. One can typically tell very quickly if a prospective mentee is serious and invested in building this relationship by the regularity of the meetings that they initiate or attend, and by their attitude and the questions that they ask. When I discern a lack of interest or personal investment in creating a mentoring relationship, I usually let these types of mismatched arrangements dwindle off on their own over time, as they are no use to anyone and simply a waste of both of our time. For a mentoring arrangement to work, both sides have to see value in the arrangement and what the mentoring relationship can provide.

One little-discussed benefit of mentoring is the value that the mentoring relationship provides to the mentor as well. In addition to the knowledge that one is "giving back", mentoring often opens up questions that challenge the mentor's own perspectives and understanding of accepted practices. I can't tell you how many times that astute and penetrating questions from a person I was mentoring caused me to question and reexamine things that I had always considered "established fact" or forced me to look at things from a different perspective. Sometimes the simple question "But why?" in response to explaining why we do things a certain way has forced me to go back and ask others the same question. These types of self-reflective activities are always beneficial, either reinforcing strongly held beliefs or forcing me to re-look at approaching things in a new and alternative fashion. In addressing these sorts of inquiries, a good mentor may find themselves saying, "I don't know, let me check and get back to you," and then head back over to their *own* mentors to sort out the answers. In fact, the optimum arrangement for any employee is to have people under them that they are mentoring, and people above them who are their mentors. This mentoring hierarchy allows a worker to build into others, and yet have a place to go to seek help for any challenging questions that they themselves may face.

Almost everyone has something valuable that they can pass along to others, and becoming a mentor is an excellent way to build others up as well as allowing the one who is mentoring to challenge themselves in the process. Embarking on this road will not only allow you to pass on what you have learned to help others, but also to engage in a process that you will likely find to be personally rewarding as well.

Guiding Principle: Many hesitate to take on the role of a mentor, incorrectly fearing that they may have insufficient knowledge or experience. However, mentoring is much more than passing on knowledge. Mentoring is also about supporting younger workers, operating as a trusted sounding board, being able to listen to issues and concerns, and pointing them in the right direction. Serving in a mentor role often uncovers questions that challenge the mentor's own perspectives, requiring them to continue to learn and grow themselves.

CHAPTER 8

You Have to Earn It

I still remember my very first day at NASA like it was yesterday. It was a very memorable day—unfortunately, not for the right reasons.

Since I was very young, I had always wanted to work for NASA (although, to be honest, my youthful dreams were always to be an astronaut). I had started my career after college working as a research and development engineer for the Department of Defense, working on advanced development concepts. Over time, I realized that none of these concepts ever seemed to get off the drawing board and I wondered if I was doomed to spend the rest of my life never creating anything that would ever see the light of day. In my job interview at NASA's Goddard Space Flight Center, my prospective new boss told me that the flight avionics unit I would be helping to design and build would be on a spacecraft and operating in orbit within three years' time. I was immediately sold. Of course, I didn't know anything about NASA's work or culture, but I was excited to learn. I knew that the job would be a stretch for me, having never worked in this type of design leadership role before, but the branch head offering me the job assured me that they would work with me closely until I got up to speed. I was excited about the opportunity to finally work for NASA so, with these assurances, I accepted the position.

I walked in on my first day at work and met my new officemate. He was about my age and obviously very sharp. I learned later that he was a brilliant electronics designer and sort of the de facto "leader" of a talented group of young designers who I would be leading in the development of a new, state-of-the-art spacecraft flight avionics unit.

The first sign of trouble came when an engineer walked into the office as I was settling in. As I introduced myself, the man looked me over from top to bottom and said, "*You're* the guy who took this job?" He shook his head and laughed, walking out of the room. I was stunned by this short, odd exchange and tried not to show it. Later the same day, another engineer from the team walked into our office to see my officemate, who introduced me as the new guy. Again, just like the previous exchange, this engineer looked me over and said, "Oh, so *you're* the new guy they got to take this job?" Like the first, he proceeded to laugh and walk out of the room.

I went home to my wife that evening and told her apprehensively, "I think I made a big mistake coming here."

It took me a few weeks to figure out what was going on. The team I had joined was staffed by a tightly knit group of young, sharp, and fairly irreverent engineers, with a high (very high!) standard of excellence. In addition, this group valued detailed electronics design above all else. Management had tried to get one of these talented group members to become the technical lead in the development of this flight avionics unit, but that position was seen as a "management" job, a dirty word in their tight-knit community. The culture of this team (see **"Creating a Team Culture"**) dictated that spending their days doing state-of-the-art electrical design was a person's highest calling. As a result, management was forced to find an outsider to come in and lead the technical development effort.

That's where I came in—literally. Not only was I an outsider, but I admittedly was a "newbie" and didn't know much about the work they were doing. And, worst of all, I wore a tie (in an ill-fated attempt to make a good impression in my new job).

I was stuck in a difficult situation. As they say at NASA, failure wasn't an option. I had just started this job and there weren't many options except to press ahead, put my head down, learn the job, and try to win this team over.

To say that the next year was difficult would be an understatement. Not only was I drinking from a fire hose in trying to learn advanced technical concepts, design practices, and even acronyms at a pace that made my head spin, I was also aware of the subtle derision from various members of the team that I was attempting to lead. Every time I asked a question that they thought I should already have known the answer to, I could see the eyes rolling and heads shaking, essentially confirming to the team that I didn't belong there. But I held my tongue, thanked the team for their patience, and moved forward. To be fair, they weren't wrong—I was a newbie, I did have a lot to learn, and, worst still, despite all this I was in charge. Even though I didn't like it, I could understand how they felt. But I was determined to learn and become a solid contributor and a good leader of the team I had been assigned to.

As I said, it was a tough year. I'm not sure exactly when it happened, but, at some point, the head shaking and the eye-rolling slowly started to diminish. I specifically recall, after roughly a year, one of the more irreverent engineers in the group turned to me after a meeting and said bluntly, "Y'know, the people in this group are realizing that you're not as big a loser as we originally thought you were." Left-handed compliment withstanding, I realized I had finally arrived.

To those of you reading this, it may seem like this team demonstrated rude and unacceptable behavior, and I can certainly understand that perspective. But I saw it differently, even back then. This was a small, tight-knit team, with obviously high standards for their work. I could see that this was one of the best design groups at Goddard and this was true for a reason. They held themselves to a very high bar in their performance and, subsequently, held me to a high bar as well, especially if I was coming in to lead their group of high performers. I didn't see it as the team members trying to be rude or mean, just expecting the same high standards that they required of themselves.

We eventually completed the design and delivery of that flight unit to the spacecraft, the X-Ray Timing Explorer, where it successfully operated for 15 years in orbit before it was decommissioned. This extended operational period was 13 years beyond its original design life, providing a glimpse of the high-reliability design and successful test program provided by our team—and not just our high-performing group, but the entire mission team. What's more, the design team that had been so challenging to join eventually became some of my most valued and trusted co-workers, who I recruited again and again to work with me on subsequent missions, and who I often sought out when I faced some of the most difficult technical challenges throughout my career (see **"Building Your Community"**).

Through this challenging process, I learned the hard way that respect is earned, not bestowed. It doesn't happen overnight, it takes patience and understanding, but the results are often worth it in the end.

Not everyone thinks this way. Some people, often those who hold senior leadership positions, mistakenly believe that their senior roles should inherently bestow respect and admiration for those who hold them. This is false. While a lofty position may, out of a sense of decorum, cause people to treat those who hold it with an outward veneer of respect, that is not the same as true respect and admiration, which is always earned. Unfortunately, people confuse this all the time.

I have another story that hammers this point home, one that didn't turn out quite so well.

On another mission, our mission development team was under the gun and working to complete our spacecraft, pushing hard to meet an aggressive schedule. NASA spacecraft development missions are rarely simple and are often constrained by cost and schedule, which can lead to tough delivery deadlines and technical delays. With this in mind, as usual, we were behind schedule, facing a number of issues, and trying to meet our rapidly approaching launch readiness date. Our management, in a seriously ill-advised decision, felt that our team needed "help" and assigned an outsider to our tightly knit team at the 11th hour with the idea that additional "management pressure" would somehow speed things up.

It didn't go well. Our team, who had worked closely together for years, and who were tired and valiantly trying to make up schedule time in the face of unexpected last-minute challenges, were suspicious of this 11th-hour "savior". The senior manager assigned to give us this "help", who was unfamiliar with our team or our mission, was placed in an impossible situation and tried to hit the ground running without taking the time to really get to know the team or the challenges we were facing. Frustrations grew. Tempers flared.

Certain members of the team did little to hide their dissatisfaction and their derision of the manager's lack of knowledge about the mission, similar to the gauntlet I had faced in my early days at NASA with my new team. This led to steadily increasing tensions within the project which threatened to boil over. Finally, in one fateful morning meeting, the manager's frustration peaked. He pointed at the assembled team and exclaimed loudly, "I'm in charge here. You *WILL* respect me!"

That was it. The team's attitude toward this manager rapidly degraded. Mocking nicknames were assigned and whispered behind his back, and any thin veneer of civility was gone. The manager, realizing he had lost the team, eventually transferred off the project.

While I don't agree with how the team responded, I understand why the situation degraded in this fashion. I firmly believe that the manager was not a bad person—on the contrary, from what I could tell, the exact opposite was true. He certainly was placed in a difficult situation. On top of this, he just didn't understand team dynamics, that true respect is earned, and it is earned slowly by working alongside the team and in the trenches, side-by-side with the people you are leading (see **"I Can't Hear What You're Saying, Your Actions Are Speaking Too Loudly"**). This can be a long, laborious process, as I had learned years earlier, but an essential one that true leaders understand.

Guiding Principle: True respect is always earned. It is never bestowed by a position or title, but only by working alongside the team and winning the respect of the people you are leading and working with.

CHAPTER 9

Drawing the Line

There is a common falsehood that is prevalent in the workplace, one that suggests that negative, belittling, and even borderline abusive behavior can somehow be an acceptable part of the workplace environment, especially when it comes down from those in leadership or management positions. Those who are accepting of this type of workplace misbehavior usually find ways to attempt to excuse or even reframe this negative behavior. Often this type of negative behavior is downplayed as an aggressive personality or management style or some other deflecting explanation. These excuses simply mask another commonly accepted workplace lie that abusive and disrespectful behavior is somehow okay in a workplace environment. The reality is, it's not.

I know of many people who have endured workplace environments that ranged from difficult to borderline hostile. In fairness, identifying a negative workplace environment can be hard to do, especially when you're in the middle of it. Most employees simply hope to ride out their difficulties, especially when there is a mismatched power dynamic because a more senior leader is the cause of the negative environment. How to respond appropriately in these types of challenging circumstances is always difficult to determine.

I can certainly relate to these types of toxic workplace environments. I was once on a job where the environment was sufficiently challenging that, even though it was difficult, I felt compelled to draw the line.

The mission we were currently working on at the time was formulated at the height of NASA's "better, faster, cheaper" phase, where missions were encouraged to push technology beyond what was currently available, while also significantly accelerating the development schedule and doing it all at reduced cost. This was before it was widely recognized that, when it came to "better, faster, cheaper", one could realistically only choose any two out of the three options without seriously risking mission success.

With these marching orders, our team accepted the challenge and plowed ahead. I still recall the "pep talk" from NASA headquarters, challenging our project team to push to implement new technology in the mission design and push it *hard*. We were told that if our team was not "*white-knuckled and sweaty-palmed*" on launch day out of fear of failure, it meant we had not pushed the technology envelope on our mission hard enough.

As a result, our team had incorporated a number of new and advanced technologies into our spacecraft design. However, there were predictable consequences to this approach. As often occurs, some of these technologies and advanced components were facing serious technical challenges and were late. As a senior technical lead on the project, I was responsible for many of them. Needless to say, in the face of technical challenges and slipped schedules, everyone on the team was extremely stressed, overworked, and exhausted.

The stress appeared to hit Todd, one of our managers, particularly hard. Todd was a good leader and excellent at his job. However, while everyone was tired and irritable due to the intense pressure we were under, Todd seemed to show it the most. His demeanor and the way he treated the team was becoming a problem. More than once I and other members of the team had to hold our tongues at the caustic comments that he would direct our way in our weekly meetings. Everyone on the team was pushing themselves to the limit to solve problems and bring in the schedule, but Todd seemed to focus only on the schedule deficit that was not being closed and not on the exhausted state of the team. I was a regular recipient of his increasingly harsh criticisms, since most of the new technologies (which were late) were under my responsibility—and I was growing weary of what I saw as unwarranted and public criticism.

At one of our team meetings, Todd singled me out yet again in front of the team and leveled his harshest, most direct criticisms yet. The rest of the team lowered their heads, averting their eyes at the onslaught. I was stunned but held my tongue. I knew a line had been crossed and something needed to change. I could understand criticism if I was not doing my job, but I was working harder than ever, even at great personal sacrifice to myself and my family, attempting to pull in the schedule. I could not see anything more that I could do other than what I was currently doing. After being pushed to the limit, I knew what I had to do next.

I was waiting at Todd's office door when he arrived early the next morning. He was surprised and a bit nervous when he saw me, perhaps realizing that he may have crossed the line the previous day.

Getting right down to business, I politely told Todd that, after the previous day's outburst at our team meeting, it was clear to me and to the entire team that he was unhappy with me and my performance. As a result, I was giving the project my two weeks' notice, after which I would be leaving and transferring elsewhere within our NASA Center. This should give the project sufficient time to find a replacement that could do my job in a more satisfactory manner.

It was Todd's turn to be stunned. He furiously backpedaled, exclaiming that he was delighted with my work and couldn't understand how I could think otherwise. It was the beginning of a long and very direct conversation about respect, how people should be treated, and how we were going to proceed moving forward. I appreciated Todd's efforts to reestablish a positive working relationship. At the end, I went back to the project and retracted my resignation, Todd agreed to monitor his behavior and public criticisms, and we both agreed to move forward.

I would love to tell you that this story ended with no more conflicts. Sadly, that was not the case. Over the course of the rest of the mission, I had to put in my resignation two more times due to similar behavior that I felt had again crossed the line, giving you an idea of the stressful environment on the project. I eventually finished the mission, but walked away much wiser and with many lessons learned.

In a previous chapter (see **"You Have to Earn It"**), we discussed how respect is earned and how this may take time and effort. However, sometimes there are extreme cases when workplace behavior may become unhealthy, or even toxic or abusive, and cannot be tolerated. It may be hard to see the difference between this and "earning respect", especially when an individual is currently in the middle of a difficult situation and trying to understand exactly what is going on. It is important to identify cases of an unhealthy workplace environment and deal with them, one way or another. As my mother used to tell me when I was younger, "If you don't respect yourself, no one else will either."

All of us have had challenging interactions with co-workers or those in positions above us, which are a reality in any workplace environment. Not all difficult situations require "drawing the line". Sometimes things are said under stressful conditions or in the heat of the moment that need to be put aside. Having worked for many years in a spacecraft development environment, I've seen it all. This is often a very dynamic and stressful environment, with tired and overworked people working in close proximity to each other and occasionally rubbing each other the wrong way. As a result, I've learned to develop a thick skin, let certain circumstances and comments roll off me, and practice tolerance and forgiveness. However, in rare cases where communications or actions of others cross the line into disrespect or extreme behavior, a line may need to be drawn. When these types of actions or behaviors consistently occur, something may need to be done. Leaders need to be on the watch for circumstances like this and be willing to step in and take action, otherwise an unhealthy or toxic culture may take root (see **"Creating a Team Culture"**).

It is important to undertake some honest self-reflection here as well. Is any criticism being directed toward you valid, however painful it may feel? No one likes to feel the sting of criticism or correction, but there have been many times in my own career when, if I was honest, it took the pointed observations of others to show me areas in which I needed to change. While we might wish that all corrections would be presented in a soft and gentle manner, this doesn't always happen. In a perfect world, healthy feedback should incorporate the following pattern—praise publicly, critique privately. Unfortunately, we don't live in a perfect world.

As previously mentioned, it is difficult to discern if the situation you find yourself in the middle of is a case of "earning respect" and receiving reasonable criticism and correction, or whether it has strayed into an unhealthy situation that needs correction. This is where bringing in someone else to assist you in evaluating the situation can be invaluable. Seek out a trusted and independent source to help you assess and obtain an independent evaluation of the situation. This is where a mentor can be invaluable in providing valued advice and helping to chart a path forward (see **"The Value of a Mentor"**).

The workplace can be challenging enough, particularly in high-profile situations with technical challenges and challenging deadlines. It is important not to add to this by allowing an unhealthy workplace that impairs a team's performance, creates a disruptive or toxic workplace environment, or drives team members away.

Guiding Principle: No job should be an excuse for abusive behavior. When facing potentially unhealthy or toxic workplace situations, you may need to extract yourself if things persist. A trusted confidant or mentor will help you assess the situation to determine any changes or next steps you should take.

CHAPTER 10

Crawl Before You Walk, Walk Before You Run

Some people believe that an individual should never turn down a promotion or advancement opportunity, even if the job in question may exceed their current experience or skill level. Promotion opportunities come along so rarely, we're told, that you should grab them while you can because you never know when the next one will come along. If you're concerned that the new position may exceed your current abilities, don't worry—you can always "grow into" a new job.

Unfortunately, this is a lie, one that has derailed and shipwrecked countless promising careers. It's also one that nearly derailed my own career when I was a young engineer.

Prior to joining NASA, I started my engineering career fresh out of college working as a research and development (R&D) engineer for the Department of Defense. Our organization had a number of R&D projects to work on, and it was a great opportunity early in my career to work in the lab, learning basic electronic design skills.

I was young, energetic, idealistic, and hungry to learn. After a few years, I must have impressed someone because I found myself in positions of greater and greater responsibility. I felt that I had landed on the fast track to advancement.

One day, I was offered what appeared to me a major career assignment to work with a team on an advanced missile system. Without much thought, I immediately signed on. After all, it would be foolish to turn down an assignment with promotion potential. Again, it seemed like my career was moving forward at a rapid pace.

I realized only later that the position was working as a liaison to a major multibillion dollar defense contractor, providing independent government monitoring of their advanced missile system development and testing. There was just one problem—I had little to no working experience in the assignment I had been given. My management needed someone in this role and, apparently, I had impressed them with my initiative and promise, but no one seemed to realize (or care) that I didn't have the experience needed for the job (or they were just looking for a "warm body" to fill the role). Very quickly, I realized that I was in way over my head, and the contractor team I was "overseeing" knew it too. Rather than being a solid contributor like I had been earlier in my career, my lack of knowledge and experience relegated me to being an ineffective observer lurking in the background. I had risen too fast and mistook advancing my position with advancing my knowledge, causing me to land in a position that I was unqualified for. I was far enough out of my element that I knew, even over time, I would not be able to grow the skills that would allow me to meaningfully contribute or be effective in this position.

It took me a while to slowly work my way out of that job position, but I made it my mission to do so. Never again, I promised myself, would I let the temptation of rapid career advancement lure me into a position that I was not qualified for.

Although this story is humbling for me to share, I do so intentionally to warn against a trend I see more and more these days, one that I have seen ruin more bright young engineering talent than anything else I have encountered. That trend is to identify bright engineers who are full of promise and move them prematurely into positions of responsibility that outpace their growing engineering skills and experience. The engineers find themselves in over their heads and often have a hard time catching up and fitting into their roles. Sadly, these once-promising people end up being ineffective in these roles, and their careers either stalled or shipwrecked. This harmful trend is not just occurring in the engineering world, but in other professions and workplaces as well.

A mentor of mine used to regularly remind me of the importance of "crawling before you walk, walking before you run." His goal was to emphasize the importance of careful, progressive steps forward, with each step building on the previous one in order to successfully reach a goal. He would apply this methodical approach to many different areas, from the careful development of a mission concept, to the methodical steps in checking out a spacecraft while in orbit. By following a thoughtful, deliberate methodology, each successive step builds on the one previously executed to create a clear path to mission success while reducing risk.

This step-by-step philosophy is just as applicable for growing people as well. Wise leaders and experienced technical people know that there is a progression of skills and experience in building a good engineer. As previously described, each career development step builds on the previous assignment and the skills developed there, leading a bright, promising, and motivated person toward establishing the set of skills needed for a successful career. Too often, though, we try to short-circuit this process, mistaking future promise for current experience and expertise. This often leads us to prematurely place people into positions that they are not ready for. There are reasons why this occurs. Perhaps a manager is short of qualified personnel and feels that they have no choice but to put an underqualified or untested employee in a role that they may not yet be prepared to undertake. Perhaps the hope is that a promising employee will rise to the challenge and succeed. The problem with this "sink-or-swim" approach is that, while some employees do rise to the occasion and "swim", too many others "sink" and suffer serious setbacks. This is unfair to the employee and is, in my opinion, poor leadership and bad management.

We ruin people when we promote them too rapidly, not giving them the opportunity to truly learn and advance in a methodical fashion. We take promising and talented workers and do them a grave disservice by advancing them too rapidly, without allowing them to truly learn the foundational skills that they need. Some do survive, but many don't. As I consider my time at Goddard, I know of too many examples where promising talent was cut short by pushing promising individuals forward without giving them the chance to learn the necessary skills required to truly advance and contribute. Typically, this is done because shortsighted managers either don't understand the need to properly grow people or, as in my case at the beginning of this chapter, there may be a "hole" that needs to be filled and they carelessly fill it without considering the consequences. Implementing a thoughtful, measured career development plan for a promising employee may take time, but this approach better prepares them by building the essential technical and experiential foundations needed to succeed. This type of approach certainly takes longer, and there is the risk that bright, promising, and ambitious young engineers may feel unnecessarily held back through this process. However, my experience has convinced me that this approach works better in the long run. It demonstrates that the organization truly cares for and takes care of their emerging star workers, even if they may feel held back.

Sometimes we characterize this as "paying your dues" before advancing. Let me be clear—I am *not* an advocate of the need to "check the box" and wait in line before progressing in your career. I *am* a strong advocate of a strong, step-by-step training process. This type of intentional process provides opportunities to progressively grow through increasingly challenging assignments, with the goal of intentionally developing the next generation of technical leaders and managers.

Most of us have heard of the "Peter Principle", which suggests that most people rise within an organization to their level of incompetence. Sadly, there is a great deal of truth to this axiom, and it is linked to the failures we are discussing. In essence, the Peter Principle warns that people are promoted based on their success in previous jobs. As long as they are successful, they will continue to be promoted upwards into roles requiring greater skill and responsibility. At some point, there is a risk that an individual will be promoted into a position where they have exceeded their training and experience and no longer have the necessary skills and ability to do their job effectively (like my early career example). At that point, they are unpromotable but now are stuck in a position where they are no longer successful. Sadly, over the course of my career, I have seen too many examples of good people who advanced too quickly and eventually ended up stuck, promoted beyond their ability to effectively do their job, and stagnated there.

Good organizations address this problem by ensuring that they have a solid training program, where talented and promising people are provided assignments with steadily increasing technical and leadership responsibilities. I have seen many excellent examples of this in some of the key engineering discipline organizations at Goddard. They develop young engineers and build technical and leadership skills through a series of work assignments of increasing difficulty and responsibility. Each successive job assignment is designed to build skills and fill experience deficits that the candidate needs addressing. It is no coincidence that those organizations have the deepest benches of senior, skilled engineers, as well as a strong mentoring program in place. In addition, leaders and managers need to be proactive in monitoring employee performance, provide coaching and support to ensure that employees in new assignments are set up to succeed, and be willing to step in at the first signs that an employee is in over their head.

Admittedly, it is difficult to ignore the lure of quick advancement when it is offered. This is especially true for younger people who are not yet sufficiently experienced to see the warning signs of where a "too-good-to-be-true" job assignment may be heading. But this rapid promotional approach often short-cuts essential skill development needed for a vibrant career. From my experience, talented people taking a slower but progressive development path eventually catch up, and they do so with experience and well-grounded technical skills that others lack. In many cases, their solid foundations result them in surpassing others later in their careers.

One notable example of this is a young engineer I worked with years ago on a previous program. It was obvious to me, from the moment I met her, that Mary was a bright and promising talent. She demonstrated a great hunger and aptitude to learn, and constantly distinguished herself by taking on progressively greater responsibility and impressing everyone around her. She entered into a technical development program at Goddard and I was assigned as her mentor. She thrived in this program and was later offered numerous outside assignments based on her obvious skills and promise. But she chose instead to stay in the program, determined to learn, grow, and build her skills. Through some unfortunate quirks in the promotion process, she lagged behind some of her peers in advancements and promotions. As she watched others advance and pass her by, she openly wondered to me if she had made a mistake by not seeking quick advancement rather than focusing on developing foundational skills through assignments of ever-increasing difficulty. Still, she was determined to stay the course. Eventually, her promotions caught up and today she is seen as a rising star and a valued technical lead for a high-profile NASA mission. More importantly, she is well-respected by her technical peers and within Goddard, and has positioned herself well for a bright and promising career.

If you find yourself in a situation where you feel that you may have landed in a position that you may not be ready for, it is never too late to change direction. It is better to readjust and work with your organization to properly learn the skills needed to effectively do your job than to continue to toil away in a position where you don't feel that you are a strong contributor. Any readjustment will help you recalibrate your career path, set a firm foundation for moving forward, allow you to move into an assignment better suited to your current skills, and help you chart future career choices.

Guiding Principle: Resist the urge to advance too quickly in pursuit of positional career advancement that gives you a title and a promotion instead of actual training. Instead, take the time to learn the foundational skills necessary to truly prepare yourself for future assignments and challenges. Workers who move forward too quickly without developing the requisite skills needed often find themselves victims of the "Peter Principle" and are unable to effectively contribute in the workplace.

CHAPTER 11

Wherever You Go, There You Are

When the home phone rings at 2 am, it is rarely good news. In this case, the news was unquestionably bad.

Our team was in the middle of a flight thermal vacuum test. This is a multiweek 24/7 test where the flight unit is sealed in a large chamber with thick airtight walls and the air is pumped out to simulate the vacuum of space. The temperature inside the test chamber is cycled through numerous hot and cold extremes to simulate the harsh spaceflight environment, all while the flight unit is operated and carefully tested and monitored. One of the toughest tests that a flight unit is subjected to, this harsh environmental test serves as the final "proof of the pudding" on whether a flight unit is ready to go into space. It is designed to reveal any hardware or design issues, such as a latent parts issue, a manufacturing or assembly flaw such as a bad solder joint, or circuit timing margin issues. It is a crucial test, as the team would prefer to find and correct any anomalies on the ground rather than be unpleasantly surprised by a failure in orbit. If something was going to fail or go wrong, this is where it will likely happen.

Within 45 minutes of my 2 am phone call, I had gotten dressed, hurried into work, and was at the test chamber. A key test had apparently failed, meaning something had gone wrong with our flight unit. The timing couldn't have been worse. We were within hours of finishing vacuum testing and, after months of hard work, were on the verge of finally delivering this long-awaited flight unit to the spacecraft. Now all of that was in jeopardy. We had an unexplained anomaly, which would mean an undefined amount of time to troubleshoot the problem. After doing this, we would likely take the flight unit back to the lab and disassemble it to locate and repair the problem. Once we were able to track down and solve the problem, which would likely mean repair and rework, we would be starting the test program all over again on the repaired unit. This process could result in a schedule slip of a month or more. It was like we had fumbled the ball just short of the goal line. The mood of the team was grim.

As I was quietly lamenting our bad fortune, a trusted electrical technician (who had been on duty during the test) quietly motioned to me and pulled me aside. Privately, the tech shared that he had observed that Brad, the engineer conducting the test on the midnight shift, may have skipped some test steps. It was possible that this "anomaly" could be an operator error rather than an actual flight unit anomaly.

Test teams are typically assigned to work in pairs so that they could assist each other and monitor the test together to prevent inadvertent errors. For this test shift, I had paired this trusted technician with Brad, a late addition to our team who had recently transferred from another group. As a new addition to our team, I was watching Brad closely, trying to determine what kind of worker he was. The test engineer position he was assigned to was extremely straightforward—all he had to do was carefully follow the step-by-step instructions that had already been defined and verified through previous testing. Now I was being given information that perhaps Brad had been a bit careless and deviated from the carefully laid out test procedure.

I wondered if part of this carelessness might have occurred because he was unhappy with the assignment he had been given. Like many young engineers, Brad was energetic and was anxious for assignments to help him advance up the career ladder. As a newer member of the team, I had intentionally assigned him to flight unit testing to check out his skills and his work ethic (see **"Crawl Before You Walk, Walk Before You Run"**). This would provide an opportunity for me to assess his performance before we assigned him greater responsibilities. Brad was very unhappy with this assignment and made no effort to hide the fact that he felt underutilized and was destined for greater things. He wanted more advanced assignments and felt that he was being unfairly held back, and I wondered if this unhappiness may have led to a lack of attention in conducting the test.

Fortunately, because of the type of test and the nature of the test failure, not to mention the helpful notes our observant technician had scribbled down, investigating the possibility of operator error was a straightforward task. Without going into the details of the test itself, our investigation allowed us to determine quite quickly that the test failure was indeed caused by operator error and the flight unit was fine. This was a huge relief! Thanks to the observations of the technician, we had avoided a costly and potentially risky rework process, not to mention significant delays to our flight schedule. Based on this good news, we would now be able to deliver on time to the spacecraft.

I profusely thanked our technician for his superb observational skills that saved the day and then pulled aside Brad to share with him the good news. I was totally unprepared for his response.

"I did not make an error!" Brad insisted angrily, his face darkening. "Whoever told you that is wrong." I gently corrected him, explaining that, due to the nature of the test and evidence in the test logs, there was no question that an error had been made—it was a verifiable fact with hard evidence to back it up. Rather than being upset, I encouraged him that this was a *good* thing, saving schedule time and avoiding a potentially risky rework process. I gently emphasized that we all make errors, that he shouldn't be upset or defensive, but that this was the best possible outcome.

This simply made Brad angrier and the conversation rapidly went further downhill from there. Rather than take responsibility in the face of incontrovertible evidence for what was likely a careless but unintentional error, he only doubled down more on his innocence and accused me of unfairly blaming him. He resurrected his grievance that I hadn't given him more promising assignments and cited this as further evidence of my bias against him.

I was stunned at this unexpected response. Rather than seeing the big picture and our good fortune, Brad instead denied all responsibility for his error and further deflected by claiming I was biased against him. He appeared to be completely missing the fact that we had avoided a major schedule hit and was focused instead on his own perceived lack of opportunities. Based on his poor response, I decided that this was a prime opportunity for an object lesson that would hopefully help him to reexamine his perspective and set him back on the right track.

Gently but firmly, I corrected him yet again. It was operator error, there was no question of that, and there was ample evidence in the test logs to prove this. Furthermore, I shared with him that his attitude during the potential test failure was very disappointing. Instead of being glad that we had avoided a costly and risky flight unit failure and rework process, he appeared to be fixated on his perceived "lack of opportunities" instead. Finally, I told him that there was a reason why he wasn't being given more advanced assignments—I and the other team leads weren't sure he was ready yet. We were giving him opportunities to demonstrate his readiness to move ahead, but instead of seeing the opportunities, he was making avoidable mistakes and topping this off by demonstrating an argumentative and unteachable attitude. I concluded by sharing that I would be glad to give him another chance and work with him to move past this and improve, but that was ultimately up to him. Mistakes happen, I reassured him, we all understand that. It's how we *respond* to those mistakes that matters most.

Unfortunately, the conversation didn't end well. The next day, I heard through the grapevine that, rather than considering my input, Brad was furious and didn't want to work with me again (which honestly was somewhat of a relief, since our type of work required people who could work together as a team and that didn't appear to be happening). I was disappointed that he was missing an opportunity to learn and grow from this unfortunate mistake, but that was his choice. We never worked together or had contact again.

I share this story for a reason, to highlight another lie I see in parts of the workplace. There's a line of reasoning infecting the workplace that one should never accept responsibility or blame for a mistake—to do so infers weakness. Instead, when confronted with a possible mistake or lapse in judgment, one should deny, stall, or do whatever it takes to deflect the problem until it goes away. Equally popular is the strategy to blame others without taking responsibility for their own mistakes and missteps, whether they be unintentional or not. Politicians do this all the time, and it allows many of them to ride out whatever current political storms they are facing to live to fight another day. Perhaps this is why this lie appears to be becoming more prevalent today.

In reality, this is a terrible strategy that avoids taking responsibility for one's actions, thereby preventing an individual from learning and growing from their mistakes. This is yet another lie masquerading as truth.

While this strategy may be quite effective in the political world, where the goal is to survive no matter what the cost, it is absolutely deadly in a normal workplace. In an engineering or other technical environment, where facts, truth, and honest results make the difference between success and failure, it is a recipe for disaster and mission failure.

When you fail to take responsibility (even for an honest mistake), what this really shows is that perhaps you and your character are the real problem. We have a saying in our house—"Wherever you go, there you are." Our family regularly uses this seemingly nonsensical phrase to refer to an individual seeking to change their fortunes only by changing their environment, but nothing else. A person may change their physical location and their environment when they move from one place to another, but they always bring themselves along with them when they move. So, if the problem is *you*, then changing your environment really isn't going to help much, is it? Your fortunes are not going to change with just a change in scenery. If the fundamental problem all along was an individual's attitude, behavior, or some other internal characteristic, changing the scenery around them won't make much of a difference. Wherever you go, there you are.

Over the course of my career, I have seen many people who feel that they have somehow been denied opportunities and that others have held them back. When there are problems, it's never their fault. Most of the time, the source of their problems is directly related to aspects of their own behavior, and that is what is actually causing their problems and holding them back. These types of people resist any effort to take a hard look at their own lives and actions as the causality for their situation—it is easier for them to pin the blame on others or on circumstances outside of their control. Eventually, when people like this don't get ahead, they leave, typically blaming others and looking for greener pastures in which to succeed. There's only one problem—the source of their issues is usually themselves, which they are not willing to see and change. Anywhere they go, they bring themselves, the source of their problem, along with them. This typically ensures that whatever issues they have will continue at their new assignment or location—all that has changed is the scenery around them. Wherever they go, there they are.

I recently read an excellent article that really hit home on this topic, entitled "5 Signs You're the Jerk at Work."[*] The author's premise is that, surprisingly, *you* may be the "jerk" that nobody wants to work with, but may also be completely oblivious to the fact that this is true. Most "jerks" are oblivious that they are the problem and blame it on others, according to the author, who warns that "If you think your team members are all jerks, it might be you." The author goes on to caution that, if indeed you're the "jerk at work", it is unlikely that anyone will actually tell you this. She goes on to explain that most people are very uncomfortable confronting others at work about their behavior. As a result, the "jerk at work" is typically left to themselves to figure it out.

I think everyone tends to have blind spots when it comes to seeing themselves clearly. I know that I do. More often than not, we view ourselves with rose-colored (or at least rose-tinted) glasses. In extreme cases, this incomplete or biased view of ourselves can cause us to reject meaningful feedback and become blinded to issues we have or problems we are causing. If we don't recognize this and make an effort to change, the scenery around us may change, but we always bring ourselves (and our problems) with us. Part of personal growth is developing the ability to see ourselves more clearly and identifying areas in need of change in our lives and our behavior. While some of this requires taking a good hard look at ourselves, our self-awareness can be helped by surrounding ourselves with people who are willing to challenge us and point out needed areas of growth and change.

---

[*] M. Torres, September 1, 2022, "5 Signs You're the Jerk at Work," Huffpost.com, www.huffpost.com/entry/signs-youre-jerk-at-work_l_630f6c87e4b0dc23bbedcc17.

Sometimes, a change of scenery is necessary. A fresh start, a new challenge, there are circumstances where these are advisable and may be the right course of action to take. But most of the time, the change needs to be within ourselves. In many instances, our circumstances reveal shortcomings and needs in our lives that we need to be aware of and address, either in our technical abilities or our character and the way we interact with others. Being willing to give ourselves an honest self-assessment and even listening to the input of trusted co-workers and friends is a good first step to continuing personal growth and improvement.

Guiding Principle: Too often, people blame others for their issues at work when their own behavior may be the problem. Rather than blaming others for workplace-related issues, wise individuals use challenging situations as opportunities for self-examination. Occasionally, workplace challenges may be indicators of needed areas of personal growth and can serve as catalysts for helpful changes in professional or personal life.

CHAPTER 12

Climbing Out of the Ivory Tower

There is a common misconception that most leaders seem to have, where they naturally assume that they are engaged and well-connected to the troops who work underneath them when, in reality, this may not be the case. These leaders believe that they understand the real challenges and issues within their organizations and that they have their fingers on the pulse of everything that is going on in the ranks beneath them.

Unfortunately, from my experience, too often this is a false assumption. In many cases, as they rise through the organization, senior leaders tend to slowly grow disconnected from what is going on in the organizations they lead, hampering their ability to identify and respond to problems, as well as hampering their ability to effectively direct and manage their workers. Apparently, no one is there to tell them that they are much more disconnected from the working level than they realize. At times in my career, I've actually been quite shocked at the apparent disconnect between senior leaders in our organization and those at the working level. In fairness, it's easy to become disconnected the higher you rise up in an organization. Unfortunately, in my experience, it appears to be the rare leader who actually has their finger firmly on the pulse of the organizations they lead.

This was clearly brought home to me on one of the missions I worked on, where I was leading the entire mission team in the development of a large spacecraft design effort. We had been struggling with a nagging technical issue and, as the lead systems engineer on the mission, I was perplexed. Try as I might, I was unable to get to the bottom of our technical problem.

One afternoon, Roger, a trusted engineer and friend who was working for me on this mission, came into my office on his own initiative and closed the door. He quietly shared that this "technical" issue that I had been unsuccessfully chasing down for some time was actually due to interpersonal issues in the working relationships between key individuals on the mission team. It had gotten bad enough that the issue was affecting the free flow of information, resulting in technical issues (see **"A Failure to Communicate"**). The conflict was becoming so obvious that other working members of the team were starting to notice and it was affecting team dynamics. When Roger caught wind of it, he decided to pay me a visit to let me know.

I thanked Roger for coming to me with information and promised him I would get right on it. But I asked him why no one had told me about this, even though the problem was becoming so evident that other working members of the team were aware of it. Roger sighed and said, "Of course no one at the working level is *ever* going to approach the mission's lead systems engineer to have that kind of conversation. You're just too high in the org chart and most people working on the floor are not willing to take that kind of dramatic step."

I was taken aback. This was a major *"ah ha"* moment, the first time I realized that I had now risen to a place in the organizational chart that created real barriers in regular communication, barriers that would impede my understanding of daily issues on the work floor. After all, I had risen through the working level myself, serving in a variety of gradually expanding capacities on previous missions before arriving in my current leadership position. Even though I was now the lead engineer on a flight mission, I had always considered myself to be a "regular guy"—approachable and willing to listen to anyone. But I realized that day, like it or not, there are invisible barriers in an organization that impede honest and open communication, even for a "regular guy" like me.

Roger's visit had opened my eyes and had done me a huge favor. I realized I could no longer assume that members of my team would come to me with any of the issues that they were dealing with, just as I was admittedly reluctant to approach those above me in the higher levels of the engineering directorate or the Center. If I hadn't been friends with Roger, I probably would have never gotten to the bottom of our "technical" issue. If I wanted to hear from the working members of the team, I realized I was the one who needed to take the personal initiative to seek out the workers on the floor, ask them questions, and solicit their inputs. From that day onward, I started making a deliberate effort to "walk the floor," asking questions and listening to the answers (whether I liked them or not). Once members of the working team got used to my visits and realized that I actually wanted to hear what they had to say, it was amazing the things I learned and how much more informed I was.

This lesson should not have been a revelation to me. When I was a young engineer, I struck up a friendship with a senior manager of the engineering directorate at Goddard, and he started regularly seeking me out to talk. Every two or three months, he would give me a call, invite me into his office, and we would talk about how things were going, what I liked about my work and the organization, what I didn't like, and what areas I felt needed improvement. I learned years later that this was part of a calculated effort on his part to stay in touch with people within his organization. He regularly met with junior members of the department to gain a "boots-on-the-ground" perspective of what was really going on, a perspective that he would have never gotten from his normal regiment of daily meetings. Not only did he encourage and mentor those younger engineers like me, but this allowed him to stay in touch with what was actually going on at the working level and keep a ground-level perspective that he might have otherwise lost in his lofty organizational position.

On every project, there are various layers of workers in the org chart, all necessary to accomplish the job at hand. There are the people who are in charge and the people who actually do the day-to-day hands-on work. The problem that often arises is that the layers in the org chart can create invisible barriers to open communication. The people near the top of the org chart lose touch with the workers on the bottom and the day-to-day challenges, issues, and potential solutions that these workers face. On the other hand, the people at the bottom of the org chart risk losing sight of the "big picture" and the trade space that is open to them to solve the problems that they encounter. These workers may also feel that the people on the top of the org chart really aren't interested in what they have to say, a complaint I have heard more than once. This is unfortunate, as these key workers on the floor often can tell you the most about what the problems really are, what to watch out for, and how to creatively solve nagging issues—and they will figure out quickly if you really want to listen. A team lead or senior manager who walks the floor will be far better equipped to accurately gauge the issues, understand their impacts, and formulate appropriate responses than one who stays in his office.

All of this takes initiative and intentionality. In addition, a leader seeking the input of the working-level team members actually has to value what the "boots-on-the-ground" workers have to say, and not just walk the floor as some sort of team building or public relations effort. Otherwise, that leader will just be checking the box and people will eventually see right through them and their actions. Unfortunately, many leaders will not see the value in building these types of connections with the working-level teams. But for those that do, not only will they become more well-informed, but they will also open up team communication and improve team cohesion and morale.

Guiding Principle: The higher you rise in an organization, the more likely it is that you will lose touch with the actual workers, isolating yourself from vital technical details and valuable "boots-on-the-ground" inputs. A leader who takes the initiative to talk to the people who actually do the work will be far better equipped to accurately gauge the issues, understand their impacts, and formulate appropriate responses than one who stays in their office.

CHAPTER 13

I Can't Hear What You're Saying, Your Actions Are Speaking Too Loudly

It was our daily mission standup meeting, but the room was more packed than usual. The project management team had asked that all key mission subsystems be represented that day, so we knew that something was up.

One of the managers stood before the team and told us what we already knew—we were entering a critical period in our development schedule, with major tests looming in the near future. The manager was blunt—we had a lot of hard work in front of us and, as a result, the team was moving into two-shift operations to meet the tight schedule. In addition, he announced that the team would be working through the upcoming weekend and everyone was expected to be there. He made it abundantly clear that we had a long road ahead of us, and everyone needed to get ready for a tough path forward and the sacrifices that would be required.

There was an audible sigh of disappointment through the assembled team as the news sunk in and thoughts of weekend plans vanished into thin air.

A hand rose in the back of the room and one of the more outspoken (and irreverent) members of the team spoke up. "And you'll be here this weekend too, right?" he asked rhetorically (or so he thought).

The manager paused. "Actually, my family has personal plans scheduled for this weekend, so I won't be here," he replied to the shocked room, apparently clueless to the stunning double standard he had just announced to the team. He immediately went on to his next topic, seemingly oblivious to the disbelieving looks around the room.

As surprising as this exchange sounds, this actually happened. That day, whatever remaining respect this manager had as a team leader was lost, and I suspect that he didn't even realize it. As bad as this was, this is probably not the most insensitive and clueless leadership example that I have witnessed in my career.

Unfortunately, there are not enough pages in this book to share the stories I have seen over my career of poor and tactless leadership. Some of them are truly shocking, such as when leaders hold themselves to one standard, then impose another more stringent standard on those working under them. This disconnect is always readily apparent to the team, whose opinion of management drops dramatically and team morale suffers.

This "do as I say, not as I do" mindset reflects another common falsehood in the workplace that needs to be called out and debunked. This mindset, typically prevalent among out-of-touch leaders, suggests that leading by example is really not that important. These types of "leaders" mistakenly believe that their senior positions somehow make them exempt from the scrutiny of those working under them. They appear to believe that they can conduct business how they see fit without considering how their actions and example may influence those serving in their organization. They mistakenly assume that being in charge and having the ability to direct their subordinates should be sufficient to effectively run the organization, regardless of their own personal conduct. This is completely false and is a striking example of poor leadership. If a leader directs their employees to do one thing, yet personally does not demonstrate this in their own behavior, they will quickly lose the respect of the team they are leading. This truth should be patently obvious, yet this example of poor leadership is shockingly common.

While poor leaders can actively destabilize a team, a good leader can serve as the "glue" that binds a team together and unites them even under adverse circumstances to achieve their goal. Such leadership encourages a team by setting an example that motivates and positively challenges the group, enabling the team to rally and move forward in a manner that would not be possible without inspirational and enabling leadership. When a leader leads by example, they model the type of behavior they want to see in their team by actively demonstrating excellence themselves. Under this type of leadership, an example is set, morale is boosted, and the team is better and more effective because of the leadership guiding them forward.

I have been fortunate enough to serve under some amazing leaders who have challenged and inspired me and facilitated my career and the success of the projects I have worked on. A common trait that these leaders have in common is an understanding that their actions and examples set the tone and direction for the team. These types of leaders know that their team's perception of their leadership has an indelible impact on the team and its morale. As a result, these leaders make an effort to lead through their example and seek to motivate their teams by being the hardest worker and setting a standard for others to follow. They understand the principle that *"more is caught than taught"*, that their example speaks much more loudly than their words ever will.

I recall one mission I worked on when the team faced a number of challenging circumstances at the launch site that threatened to derail and splinter a tired and worn-out team. The project manager, knowing the state of the team, lived and worked among them at the launch site in such a manner as to resurrect a worn-out team and lead them through the challenges and to a successful launch. If you were to poll the members of the team afterward (and I did), to a person they would tell you that they would have never been able to achieve what they did without the persistent and unifying efforts of that project manager.

There have been innumerable books written on the nature of leadership and what constitutes a good leader (and a poor one). There's no way I could possibly cover this topic as effectively as others have done. However, there are a few striking leadership characteristics that I have seen over my years at NASA that are worth sharing. Good leaders lead from the front, not from behind, and lead by example. They know their project's or organization's goals and keep the team laser-focused on what's important and how to get there. They work hard to know their team well in order to effectively lead them. They know what makes the members of their team tick and what motivates them and have their finger on the daily pulse of their team. They have earned the respect of the team, and the team is willing to follow their leadership wholeheartedly. This last one is likely the most important. If no one is really following you, are you really a leader? Good leaders tend to have their pick of good people because others are willing to follow them from project to project because of their excellent leadership and because they are admired and trusted.

This type of leadership approach has a trickle-down effect on the team that serves under them, causing many of the other team members to emulate their example. This process of a leader setting the tone and those under them following in their footsteps to mimic their leadership example is one of the essential steps in establishing a team culture that eventually takes root and guides the entire team (see **"Creating a Team Culture"**).

While good leaders adhere to the philosophy of leadership by example, there unfortunately seems to be no shortage of poor leadership examples. I have seen innumerable examples across the course of my career of gaffe-prone and insensitive leadership, where leaders did not lead by example and were often unaware of this shortcoming. Whatever guiding words they may have hoped to share were completely overshadowed by the poor example that they set. All leaders are actively creating a team culture, whether they realize it or not, and poor leaders create a culture that reflects their poor leadership style. The resultant culture of poor leaders is often problematic and in need of serious repair. The people in organizations like these do not actually "follow" their leaders but often silently endure while working underneath them.

A common denominator that many of the cases of poor leadership seem to have in common is an "insular" leadership approach, where there is no opportunity for the leader to receive outside feedback. Such feedback might actually serve as a catalyst to trigger some honest self-evaluation of their leadership effectiveness (see **"Avoiding Blind Spots"**). Either intentionally or unintentionally, many poor leaders have cut off avenues for others to provide them with input that would provide warning signs of the effects of their leadership style. This type of leadership is typically defined by a lack of accountability, and is often missing loyal yet honest deputies who are empowered to "tell it like it is". In most of these cases, these roles either do not exist or the deputies have been cowed into submission where they feel that they cannot give their honest assessment without retribution or retaliation. This leaves their failing leader blissfully oblivious to the detrimental impact that their poor leadership is having on the people and organization around them. In fact, it is entirely possible that such leaders may falsely see an absence of critical feedback as indications of their successful leadership. Sometimes the organization adapts and learns to survive despite the poor leadership—oftentimes it does not.

The opposite is true of effective leaders. These types of leaders actively seek out feedback from others, even when it may be difficult to hear. They recognize the likelihood that those underneath them are often reluctant to give them feedback (see **"Climbing Out of the Ivory Tower"**), so they take the initiative on their own to seek out feedback to improve their performance and leadership. These types of people work hard to surround themselves not with "yes men", but with people who will give them brutally honest feedback that they might not want to hear. These types of leaders realize that honest feedback is beneficial to them and to their organization.

Everyone wants good leaders, but actually becoming one can be very challenging, which is why good leadership is so hard to find. Good leadership does not happen by accident, but requires intentionality. It requires self-awareness, hard work, an ability to examine oneself closely, a respect for the team working for you, and a willingness to lead by example and solicit honest feedback. For those who are willing to undertake this challenging path, the personal rewards and the benefits to their teams are certainly worth the effort.

Guiding Principle: Good leaders know that they lead by the example that they set. As a result, they hold themselves to stringent standards and work hard to actively seek feedback from trusted deputies on their leadership style and effectiveness. The example they set flows down through the team and helps set the culture of the organization. As a result, they earn the respect of the teams that they lead.

CHAPTER 14

Creating a Team Culture

The first time I was assigned as the lead Mission Systems Engineer on a flight mission, I adopted a practice that helped me immensely in assessing and evaluating our systems engineering team and identifying any areas where we might need to change.

About three months after a new member would join our systems engineering team, I would invite them into my office, close the door, and encourage them to share with me any observations they had gathered thus far about our team. This would typically elicit puzzled looks until I would explain to them why I was doing this and what I hoped to gain from it.

What I was hoping to obtain was a clear, unvarnished look from an outsider's perspective of our team, how we operated, and any specific observations that they noted. In my opinion, three months is enough time for a newcomer to become sufficiently immersed in the team in order to see it clearly, but not long enough for the newness required for these types of observations to wear off. I wanted to get a glimpse, from an outsider's perspective, of what they thought the culture of our team was, with an eye toward constantly working to improve our team and how we worked together.

Going through this process, I would always learn something. Most of the time, the comments I received echoed my own observations about our team and its culture. Sometimes, I was surprised by an observation that I had completely missed. I always felt that these exchanges were incredibly valuable. In almost every instance, once my visitor warmed up, they seemed to really appreciate the opportunity to provide their inputs and observations.

Many people don't realize that every team has a unique culture—an unwritten philosophy of how the team works, communicates, and interacts internally and with people outside the team. There are numerous myths and misunderstandings surrounding the idea of a team's culture that often need to be corrected. One of the biggest myths is the belief that every team or organization doesn't necessarily have a distinct team culture (they do). Those who accept the idea that there is a culture unique to their team may believe that it is developed organically and can't be influenced or directed in any meaningful way (it can). Some believe that culture is mainly about interpersonal interactions and doesn't really affect the way an organization works and doesn't impact an organization's effectiveness or work output (it does).

A team's culture represents what a team truly values and, as a result, helps define its work ethic, its attention to detail (or lack thereof), how well (or poorly) people are treated, whether questions are openly asked (or discouraged), whether the team is detail (or "big picture") oriented, and how the team approaches troubleshooting and problem-solving. Some teams are meticulous, some more casual, some very process-oriented, others less rigid, some open to give-and-take discussions, others more regimented in their communication. Many teams may be unaware that their culture even exists, or that it can influence mission success. Even at Goddard, different projects working at this same NASA Center often have widely different team cultures. If you consider the organizations you have been part of, it shouldn't be hard to come up with a list of distinctive practices that demonstrate key facets of each organization's shared culture.

Oftentimes, we *think* we know what the culture of our team is, but it is possible that we are simply deceiving ourselves. It often takes someone from the outside to truly provide a fresh and unbiased look at what our team is really like, what we value and focus on, how we interact with each other, and how we do business and get things accomplished. This is why I would regularly invite the "three-month" employees for a "culture debrief"—to conduct a regular assessment of our team and see if there was anything that needed correcting.

Unsurprisingly, the primary source for setting the tone for the team is the team's leader, who establishes the team culture and how the team operates. I learned this after observing many teams and sitting in on many design reviews for a wide variety of missions. A project typically takes on the priorities, leadership philosophy, and values of their leader. Whenever I note some unique aspect of how a project operates and wonder where this came from, I have learned not to look any further than the project's leader. More often than not, it is that leader and their core leadership team who, either intentionally or unintentionally, are the source of the team's culture.

Wise leaders understand this principle and proactively and intentionally work to create the specific type of culture that they hope to establish. A team's culture can be a powerful tool in guiding and keeping everyone marching together on the same page. It helps set the tone for new team members and reminds existing team members what is valued and keeps them properly focused. It can also create a unifying identity and a sense of pride and common purpose that assists in team cohesion.

A weak or disruptive culture can have the opposite effect. It can create a resistance to good practices, creating pockets of "groupthink" (see **"The Danger of No Dissent"**) instead of creative and critical thinking. A negative culture can even promote an "us versus them" mentality toward outsiders, one that resists outside input and the positive influence and new ideas it can bring.

While a strong and proactive leader will seek to intentionally create a culture within the team that guides the team in key principles and practices, a less informed or nonproactive leader may not. A culture will be created, nonetheless, it just may not be one that the team leader intends or would prefer.

A team's culture can also have a far-reaching effect even beyond the project in question. A positive team culture not only benefits the project itself, but often the "disciples" of that culture eventually move on to other areas and take their hard-won lessons and cultural attributes with them. Early in my career at NASA, I worked with a senior systems engineer who was meticulous in spacecraft testing and troubleshooting, and whose strength in this area contributed to the success of numerous satellites. He strongly espoused the regular use of the formal problem-reporting system to document, track, and close out issues discovered during testing. At the time, many on the engineering team were reluctant to formally document issues in the system. They preferred to document any issues that arose in a "grass roots" system rather than a formal reporting system. As long as *someone* was documenting issues, they reasoned, there was no need to be overly formal about the process. The problem with this ad hoc approach was that there was no centralized system where everyone could access and evaluate the open issues on the spacecraft and get the "big picture" of what issues were open and closed. I also suspect that part of the resistance to the formal reporting system was that documenting issues in a larger system open to everyone on the team (and other people outside the team) would give any open issues more visibility than some of the team members would prefer. It was more comfortable to deal with issues "in house" and keep them close to the vest rather than allowing others outside the team to have greater visibility into them. Some of it was laziness, some of it stemmed from the cumbersome nature of the formal system, and a large part of it was the perception that documenting a large number of problems would somehow tag our development effort as being more troubled or problematic than other missions. Fortunately, our senior engineer constantly emphasized that the problem-reporting system was a valued tool to make sure that issues were properly identified, investigated, root cause established and addressed, reviewed, and closed out in a rigorous manner. Instead of making our project seem riskier, he claimed that fully documenting issues would enhance the overall reliability of the mission and, accordingly, the confidence we and our NASA Center would have in our finished product. He worked with the project manager to actively shape the culture of the engineering team. Together, they promoted the proper use of the problem-reporting tool and actively corrected the misperceptions that formally documenting problems would mark the project as troubled. This effort changed the project engineering team culture and the manner in which we investigated, addressed, and closed out issues. Today, as I look at the engineers who "grew up" on that program and now have spread throughout Goddard, I see the fruits of that cultural change and the positive effect it still has today in helping to ensure reliable spaceflight hardware.

Always keep in mind that every team *will* establish a culture, whether it is done intentionally or is allowed to occur "accidentally" without a guiding hand to direct it. It is up to the leader to determine how the culture will be established, and whether they will take active steps to define and steer the culture on a path that best benefits the team and the mission goals.

Guiding Principle: Every team has a unique culture that distinguishes them from others and guides how well (or how poorly) they do business. Proactive leaders do not leave culture building to chance, but intentionally work toward building a culture that unites the team on a clear path toward mission success.

CHAPTER 15

The Danger of No Dissent

On January 28, 1986, the Space Shuttle Challenger took off from Kennedy Space Center Launch Complex 39B, the 10th flight for the orbiter Challenger and the 25th overall flight of the entire Space Shuttle fleet. Seventy-three seconds later, disaster struck as the shuttle broke apart in flight, killing the crew of seven, which included the first teacher assigned to fly into space. Subsequent investigation revealed the cause of this accident was a breach in the primary and redundant O-ring seals in the shuttle's right solid rocket booster, starting a chain of events that would lead to the disaster. The Rogers Commission, tasked with investigating the accident, came to the conclusion that the decision process that led to the launch of Challenger that day was seriously flawed.

Many who have studied the decision process, which ignored safety concerns prior to the launch, cite this as a classic case of "groupthink".

The term "groupthink" was defined by the social psychologist Irving Janis as "a psychological drive for consensus at any cost that suppresses dissent and appraisal of alternatives in cohesive decision-making groups."[*] In a groupthink environment, there is subtle and often subconscious pressure to overlook potential problems that could interfere with arriving at a common perspective or solution. In addition, if someone in the group raises an issue or concern that threatens this common point of view, the groupthink environment will apply pressure to minimize or eliminate this minority opinion or anything else that could interfere with group agreement and consensus. While a common consensus may appear to be a good thing, it should never be arrived at

---

[*] I.L. Janis. July 1, 1972. *Victims of Groupthink: A Psychological Study of Foreign-Policy Decisions and Fiascoes*, Houghton Mifflin Company.

by ignoring real issues and concerns—doing so will likely have negative consequences.

In an earlier section (see **"Creating a Team Culture"**), we discussed the importance of creating a cohesive team culture and identity where everyone is on the same page and working toward the same goals in the same manner. We admire finely tuned teams that share philosophy and culture and can almost finish each other's sentences because of their excellent teamwork. Therein lies a trap that must be avoided: becoming so well integrated that groupthink creeps in and eliminates valid opposing viewpoints. This could cause a team to miss alternative approaches or, even worse, miss hidden concerns until they become real problems. A wise leader must take pains to cultivate an environment where outside reviews and internal minority opinions are not only acceptable but actually sought out as part of the normal process of doing business.

There is a common and troublesome workplace mindset suggesting that people who raise unpopular concerns or other forms of dissent against the prevailing views in a group are somehow disloyal or even branded "troublemakers". This is a false conclusion and can lead to dangerous consequences. While it is true that any organization can have individuals who are naturally contrary and whose negative attitude can make life difficult for the rest of the team, this should never be cause for discounting valid concerns and minority opinions simply because they are inconvenient or disagree with the popular opinion at the time. Choosing not to entertain or carefully evaluate these minority opinions and alternate perspectives but instead squashing or discouraging them from being raised creates a fertile ground for the creation of a dangerous groupthink environment.

There are a number of steps that project teams can take to ensure that groupthink does not become embedded within a project team. An obvious first step is to respect and take advantage of the project's external review process. NASA has instituted mandatory independent reviews at every mission lifecycle phase and every major milestone (see **"Someone Looking Over Your Shoulder"**). There is a tendency for project teams to groan at these required reviews, but they have a valuable role in providing an independent look at a project, its technical progress, and even their decision-making process. As a flight project lead systems engineer, I and my teams worked hard to cultivate an environment where our teams took the review process seriously as a valuable tool (rather than a necessary evil) and saw our review teams as partners in developing a successful mission. On one particular mission, our project manager took this "partnership" with the review team a step further. After our design passed through the Critical Design Review, our project manager made a habit of regularly updating key review team members, briefing them on any significant issues or changes, even when these fell outside the normal review "gates." As a result, we developed a positive working relationship with our review team, helping them to be better educated in their review and assessment of our progress. We benefited from the review team's input and they benefited from being better informed on our project.

Internally, our project focused on creating an environment where the systems team regularly reviewed and questioned major design decisions and issues, with the express goal of making sure that any questions or concerns were clearly aired and not squelched or marginalized. Our weekly systems team meeting served as an anchor to ensure that honest and open discussion occurred. Frank and candid communication also occurred at other project meetings, including design and development meetings and risk meetings. As part of the team culture that we worked hard to establish, we had no shortage of people willing to challenge the status quo and take on "devil's advocate" positions. While this give-and-take discussion could sometimes be frustrating, in the end it resulted in a better team and a more reliable mission.

The dangerous thing about groupthink is that it is so subtle and insidious and can creep up on a team so slowly that they may not be aware that it is even there. A good analogy is the apocryphal story about putting a frog in a cold pot of water, then turning up the temperature so slowly that the frog doesn't realize the temperature change until it is boiled alive. Alerting a team to the dangers of groupthink keeps this concern and the dangers that it could pose at the forefront of everyone's mind. It also helps to continually emphasize vigilance in questioning decisions and results, and not adopting an overly optimistic perspective, but instead cultivating the engineer's natural skepticism at all times. As one person put it, a good systems engineer should be a "closet optimist"—secretly hoping for the best, but outwardly willing to question everything. Cultivating this trait in a project team's culture will go a long way in helping to ward off a groupthink environment.

Guiding Principle: While forming a united and like-minded team is essential to mission success, beware of "groupthink". Every leader needs to ensure that the team carefully considers all issues and concerns and entertains minority opinions, with the goal of making sure all hidden questions and concerns are brought to light and carefully considered.

CHAPTER 16

Reinventing the Wheel

Not all workplace falsehoods and deceptions are out-and-out lies. Some are quietly unhelpful and self-deceptive practices that mislead and waylay well-meaning employees without them even realizing it.

Case in point—I can recall vividly an instance where our project systems engineering team was grappling with a particularly challenging problem and we were trying to determine how to proceed. All the while, one of our project managers sat at the table, silently tapping his pencil while he listened to our team go round and round on this issue. Finally, during a lull in the conversation, he finally spoke up. "I guess no one at Goddard Space Flight Center has ever dealt with a similar issue," he said quietly, then went back to tapping his pencil.

Our team was silent, embarrassed. We immediately got his message and shifted our focus to canvassing the Goddard community to seek out anyone who might have struggled with similar issues and was able to share their experiences to help us out. It didn't take us long to get information that enabled us to address our issue and move ahead.

This somewhat embarrassing episode highlights a recurring problem on many teams: "re-inventing the wheel" rather than leveraging the work and experience of others to solve problems. This unfortunate workplace practice is defined by the *Merriam-Webster* dictionary as the tendency "to waste time trying to do something that has already been done successfully by someone else." There are a variety of reasons why this practice might occur in an organization. No matter what the cause, the result is that teams choose to forgo a proven solution in favor of starting all over again and possibly repeating mistakes that others have already learned. This practice can result in time and cost inefficiencies that could have been easily avoided.

When a team does not explore whether the work of others might help them in solving their challenges, they miss opportunities to reach out to other teams who might be able to offer much-needed assistance by providing relevant information. Engineers often spend tremendous amounts of effort trying to come up with a unique solution rather than building on the foundations of others. A wise individual I once worked for was fond of saying, "When you are in college and you copy someone else's work, it's called plagiarism, and it can get you kicked out of school. In the world of engineering, this is called good engineering practice, and it often results in awards and promotions."

There are two key reasons why teams don't seek outside assistance to solve team problems and neither of them is a "technical" challenge.

The first reason that teams tend to keep reinventing the wheel rather than seeking outside help is often a "networking" issue, where individuals on a team simply are not aware of the work that others may have done in similar areas. Being unaware of the potentially helpful work of other groups may have many possible origins—it may be the inexperience of the team, or it may be that they are "stovepiped" from other organizations and have not developed natural means of cross-communicating to learn what other organizations are doing. Because a team is lacking in networking skills and communicating with other organizations, their awareness of alternate approaches may suffer as a result, leading them to "reinvent the wheel". This behavior is typically an unintentional problem, caused by poor outside contacts or an overly insular team. A good team leader should assess their team in this area and work with the team to ensure that they build a network of contacts outside their own organization.

A second reason that contributes to this problem may be more intentional—it may be caused by a "not invented here" culture in the team. A "not invented here" mindset either intentionally or subconsciously dismisses or refuses to search out valid implementation approaches outside the home organization. This is typically caused by a resistance to approaches not conceived and developed within the team. While pride of ownership within a team is a valuable mindset, it should never be pursued at the cost of ignoring outside alternate concepts. Teams need to aggressively avoid the trap of "not invented here" that prevents them from tapping the experience of those who came before and may have valuable inputs and information to offer. The team will be the better for it and, in the process, may also further build a network of external contacts and peers, and perhaps even mentors.

Both of these impediments, possible "networking" issues and a "not invented here" culture, are clearly non-technical "people-type" issues that can directly threaten a team's technical performance, and therefore need to be addressed when they are detected by the team leader.

In order to combat the "reinventing the wheel" trap, a team needs to ensure that all alternatives, both inside and outside the team, are examined and considered. I confess that this has not always been a strong point of mine. Early in my career, I would often tend to defer to "homegrown" solutions rather than casting a wide net to investigate what others may have done and how it could help our team. Over time, I learned the immense value of examining a wide variety of solutions, both internal and external to our team. Later in my career, when leading technical teams, I would make sure that our team always asked themselves, "Who has done this type of mission before and what can we learn from them?" We made sure that our team sought out knowledgeable people from other missions and picked their brains for helpful implementation details and lessons learned. Even so, as the example at the beginning of this chapter reveals, these old habits are often hard to break. We would occasionally find ourselves in a situation where we missed obvious contacts with other missions and technical experts who, in retrospect, would have helped us tremendously. This is an excellent warning that teams need to be constantly reminded to pursue others in the community who might be able to help them with their current challenges.

A good strategy to help avoid "reinventing the wheel" is to intentionally seek out the expertise and experience of other groups and their success in solving various challenges and issues. Not only will this open up potential solutions, but will also open up networking and communication that will be beneficial to a project team.

Guiding Principle: Avoiding the trap of "reinventing the wheel" requires an intentional effort to explore whether the work of others might help in solving challenges. Teams need to make sure that they

are consciously working to network with other outside organizations for possible solutions. In addition, teams need to aggressively avoid the trap of "not invented here" that prevents them from tapping the experience of others that aid in developing solutions.

CHAPTER 17

The Right Man (or Woman) for the Job

There is a popular line of thinking that most jobs are fairly generic and, as long as a possible candidate possesses a certain set of skills, virtually anyone can do almost any job. There is no need to spend valuable time looking for the "perfect candidate" to fill a position when just about anyone with the right basic set of skills will do. A job is simply a job, after all.

This sounds reasonable—and yet in many cases is patently false. This is another untruth that doesn't match real-world experience. Taking the time to find the right candidate for a given position is one of the most important things a leader can do to set the team and the project up for success.

The effort we made in finding the right candidate for a key role on one of our spaceflight missions provides a perfect counterpoint for this widely accepted falsehood. Our flight mission was getting started and we were in the process of staffing up key positions. I had one particularly challenging role that I needed filled, one that required a unique set of technical skills that were hard to find. Fortunately, I knew just the person to fill that role. Unfortunately, Regina, the person I wanted, was finishing up another flight project and wouldn't be free for another six months (longer if there was a launch delay on her current project).

I talked to Regina and confirmed that she was interested in the position (once she was free), then told my project management that I would leave the position unfilled until she was available and that she was the one I wanted to fill this important position. This was not a popular decision with my management. They wanted the position filled as soon as possible, and I got some serious pushback. The management team was rightly concerned that filling this position late could seriously set us back, especially in the formative stages of the project when many key decisions were being made. I certainly understood this concern, but countered that having the right person in the role for the duration of the mission was worth the short-term risk. Additionally, while there were other candidates, there was no one with the expertise and experience that Regina possessed. In my opinion, she was worth waiting for. After quite a bit of back and forth, where I firmly stuck to my stated position on the matter, the project reluctantly agreed to wait and hold the job open. Later, when Regina finally arrived on the project, she quickly came up to speed and wowed the team, just as I expected. She was a huge asset to the mission development effort and an integral part of our eventual mission success.

Based on my experience, there is one key factor that has a tremendous weight in determining whether a mission is successful or not. A mission's success or failure is ultimately determined by the people assigned to the project. As a friend of mine in the spacecraft business once put it, "We spend millions of dollars on equipment and flight hardware, but, without question, the most valuable asset we have is our people." Staff a project with the right people and there will be virtually no obstacle they cannot overcome, given the proper resources. Staff a project with a less-than-optimum or dysfunctional team, and they will struggle despite receiving the necessary resources and support. Many people make the mistake of thinking that simply filling empty positions in the project org chart will lead to a project's success. This approach incorrectly assumes that people are fairly interchangeable and staffing specific roles is not of critical importance. In fact, just the opposite is true. Wise leaders realize that people, not positions, get the job done, and selecting the right people for key positions either sets a project up for success or dooms it to a wealth of troubles down the road. Selecting the right people for specific positions, roles, and responsibilities will always make the difference when challenges (technical or otherwise) hit. This may seem obvious, but it is astonishing how often some leaders are content to fill positions rather than take the time to build a team.

Anyone who has worked in a team environment can probably recall an example of a well-intentioned individual who, for whatever reason (lack of experience or underdeveloped interpersonal or communication skills, among others), was placed in a key role on a team where they were a poor fit. When a key role is staffed by someone poorly suited for the role, problems start to occur, and the rest of the team struggles to compensate for the deficiency of this underperforming team member. The team is either forced to add unplanned additional personnel to augment shortcomings in this key role or learns to "work around" the individual in question. This results in a lot of extra workarounds on the team that could have been eliminated if more care had been taken to ensure a good staffing fit early in the project. On top of this, if the deficiencies are significant, a staffing change may need to be made later, causing disruptions within the team.

Staffing key positions with optimum personnel choices sounds wonderful in a perfect world where there is an abundance of highly qualified people who are perfect for every available role. In the real world, however, there are often shortages of qualified personnel and leaders may not always have the best options for choosing their staff. In these cases, it is critical to choose rising talent that, even though they may not be an optimum choice, appears to possess the right raw materials in technical ability, attitude, and hunger to learn. It is essential that these rising stars be paired with a more experienced mentor and a good support system. This support will help to ensure that a newcomer does not fall into a "sink or swim" experience (where they may sink!), but instead one where they have clear avenues of support and go-to contacts for help and advice when they run into trouble (see **"Crawl Before You Walk, Walk Before You Run"**).

The perennial challenge of finding experienced workers means that a wise leader will always be on the lookout for skilled workers. When these leaders spot rising talent, they will quickly scoop them up when they can. A perfect example of this proactive approach occurred on one of our missions when the value of talent was recognized and used to augment the existing team. Late in the project development effort, we brought in a highly skilled individual on a targeted task to perform crucial technical reviews. This individual did an amazing job in this role and impressed me and the other members of our leadership team. After these targeted reviews were completed, rather than let this valuable individual go, I went to the project manager and requested bringing this engineer on full-time. I confessed that I hadn't thought through the specific role this individual would fill, but emphasized the principle that skilled people are rare and we should grab them first and ask questions later. Fortunately, our project manager agreed, and this engineer stayed through the rest of the project, solving many technical issues and performing as a key member of our systems team. Even though we didn't have a particular position that needed filling at the time, we saw the value of a specific individual, realized the potential benefit to the team, and grabbed him. Good people are hard to find, and you need to snap them up when you see them—you will always find ways later where they can fit in and contribute.

Staffing a project well puts in place a strong foundation for everything that follows and sets up a project for success. Good leaders understand the value of people and their essential role in mission success. Conversely, staffing issues are guaranteed to cause problems on a team and distract them from focusing on the true challenges of the mission.

Guiding Principle: Wise leaders realize that people, not positions, get the job done. Taking the time to choose the right people for key positions will set the project up for success and lower the risk of incurring problems down the road. When the optimum choice for a position is not available, make sure that anyone who is learning on the job is paired with a good mentor and support system to help them learn and succeed as they grow into their role.

CHAPTER 18

Training Your Replacement

As was so often the case, we were crazy-busy on our flight project and, at the same time, my ever-patient wife was asking me when I could take some time off to take the family on a long-overdue vacation. We were at a crunch time in building and testing our spacecraft and, as a result, the goal of meeting our flight schedule was taking priority over family events.

I vividly recall talking to my project manager about my dilemma—the urgent needs at work versus the need to take some time off with my family. I will always remember what she said to me—"John, you can take off any time you want…as long as you have someone to fill your shoes while you are gone."

A wise senior systems engineer who was a mentor of mine often reminded me that every job actually has two primary components: to do your work with excellence and integrity, and to train your replacement. Unless you have trained your replacement, he would say, you have not fully done your job.

There is a tremendous amount of wisdom captured in this advice. If you have not trained someone to step in behind you, even short departures (like my vacation scenario above) leave a "hole" that may seriously impact the organization in your absence. This inadvertently promotes an unhealthy work environment, when hard-working team members feel that they cannot take time off without hurting the project. Because they cannot take needed personal time off, there is significant potential for undue stress in their personal lives. This stress can lead to burnout and other problems. Even worse, without a fully trained replacement, an individual may find themselves trapped in their current position, since their departure for another position would leave a gaping hole. A typical way our team would reference the threat of a sudden and unanticipated departure of a critical team member is to joke about the "getting hit by the bus" scenario (as in, "I want to make sure you understand what to do here just in case I get hit by a bus"). What this dark humor is actually highlighting is the real risk of a key individual suddenly disappearing, for any reason, with the sudden loss of their skills or knowledge base leaving the team in the lurch. Good organizations realize the need for cross-training so no individual is a single-point failure, where their loss, however temporary, puts the team at a serious disadvantage.

Adopting a train-your-replacement mentality provides a clear avenue for mitigating the risk to the project that the loss of a key team member can incur. This approach also creates a fertile environment where the skills of an organization are continually replenished through mentoring and passing of the baton. Imagine an organization where there is a deliberate and intentional effort to challenge the more experienced team members to intentionally train and mentor younger members of the team. This organization would be constantly passing on valuable skills to junior employees, while also building up a "bench" in the event of unexpected absences or departures. In addition, having a "train your replacement" mindset transforms the way individuals in the team think, specifically how they view and deal with other members of their team. Time and again, I see the frustration that senior engineers may have with those who are less experienced slowly melt away as they understand the vital role they have in passing their knowledge and experience to these junior employees (see **"Be a Mentor"**). Not only does this promote open technical interchange, it also fosters a nurturing and team-building culture (see **"Creating a Team Culture"**).

I can recall a specific instance where adopting my mentor's "train your replacement" advice was extremely helpful to me personally. I was the lead systems engineer on a high-profile mission, one with significant visibility within Goddard and NASA. One of the first things I did after being appointed in my new role was to immediately select two incredibly talented deputies to work alongside me. Not only did I realize that I needed help on this challenging mission, I remembered the admonition on the need to train my replacement. I wanted to make sure that there were qualified people to take over for me if needed.

From day one, we would have regular meetings, just the three of us, to make sure we were all on the same page and that my deputies knew everything I did. I wanted to make sure that we could think and act as one as much as possible. I would constantly remind my deputies that, even though I planned to be on the project for a while, it was not a given that I would be there on launch day, and they needed to be prepared to take over in the event that one day I left. I wanted to instill the necessary long-term learning and ownership mindset needed for an eventual leadership role in the event they needed to take over for me. My goal was ensuring that the project would be in good hands if I ever decided to move on. While that was my long-term goal, my near-term goal was to make sure that they could step in for me so that I could take a vacation whenever I wanted (as my project manager so aptly pointed out in the beginning of this chapter) or to fill in for any other unexpected short-term absence. After being on the project for a number of years, I eventually decided to depart the project and move on to something new. Again, due to the high-profile nature of the mission and my role as the lead systems engineer, there was serious concern about the impact my departure might have in the middle of the mission development effort. As a result, the discussion of my potential departure was kicked upstairs to Goddard senior management for discussion, as well as to NASA headquarters. I was glad that I had worked for years to "train my replacement"—despite the concerns that were raised about my departure, I was able to clearly show that either of my new deputies was more than qualified (some would say *more* qualified!) to take over for me after my departure. In fact, I often joked that my greatest contribution to that project was leaving and replacing myself with even better leaders than I was!

The situation described above was successful and allowed me to move on because I had the foresight to develop a long-term approach to train people who could fill my shoes. Conversely, I have also seen situations where an experienced individual was blocked from taking another preferred assignment because of the "hole" that their transfer would leave in their current work assignment. The reality is, the greater the responsibility or the higher the profile that an individual's job has, the more difficult it is for that individual to move due to the impacts their departure may have on a mission or an organization's well-being. Like my case, legitimate questions on the potential impact of a key individual's proposed transfer often go all the way up the organizational chain. In some cases, however, the transfer is ultimately blocked because the departure runs the risk of hurting the current project that they are supporting. Eventually, most transfers like these are allowed to occur, but only after another skilled individual is identified and trained to allow a gap-free departure. This training and eventual replacement does not happen overnight, and it often takes a prolonged period of time for the skill transfer to occur. These delays could have been prevented if cross-training or training a replacement had taken place earlier.

It is worth mentioning that not everyone on your team may ascribe to this "train your replacement" mindset and may feel threatened by this approach. One of the conventional bits of "wisdom" that is often shared in the workplace is that teaching other people to do your job only puts your job at risk. The thinking is that, once someone else knows how to do your job, you are now replaceable… and disposable. A (non-NASA) friend of mine once shared with me his work strategy that clearly reflects this anxiety. He told me that he consciously grabs as much responsibility as possible and avoids sharing information unless absolutely necessary. His goal was to make sure no one knew how to do his job but him, making himself unique and indispensable to further ensure his job security. Certainly, that is one strategy, but one that I do not agree with and absolutely one that is not good for the team or organization. While I can see the twisted logic of this approach, I am a firm believer that demonstrating good teamwork makes you more valuable to the organization and thereby enhances your opportunities and job security.

Encouraging team members to "train their replacement" has obvious advantages across the project, both in preventing staffing holes due to temporary absences and departures, and in building a more robust and cross-trained team. Wise team leaders will encourage the members of their teams to adopt this training and team-building approach and work to make it part of their team culture.

Guiding Principle: A key part of every worker's job should include the mandate to "train their replacement". Unanticipated absences, whether they are short or long term, can create serious staffing problems on a team. Vigorously promoting a "train your replacement" mentality among the team will help avoid these types of staffing interruptions and help to create a culture of mentoring and cross-training among the team.

CHAPTER 19

Someone Looking Over Your Shoulder

One of the first steps in developing a flight project's mission concept is for the engineering team to meet with the members of the science team and define the mission requirements, which serve as the "blueprint" for the actual mission design. This effort to form a science-based mission concept is a highly iterative process and can be a long and arduous task for both sides. In a sense, both teams speak a different "language", and trying to come together to a common understanding can be extremely challenging.

It was in one of these meetings, late in the day, that one of the scientists was jotting our latest progress down on paper, with one of my systems team members looking over his shoulder. Sensing his presence, the tired scientist turned around abruptly and asked indignantly, "Are you checking my work?" The systems team member reddened and quickly stepped away.

Later, at the end of the day, I caught up to my team member and, between the two of us, recalled the incident. Before the individual could speak, I said, "You know what the correct answer to that question was, right? Your response should have been *YES*! We *always* check each other's work!"

I certainly understand this scientist's reaction. It is human nature for any individual not to appreciate someone looking over their shoulder, potentially second-guessing them and critiquing their work. However, there is tremendous value in having experienced, trusted people "double-check" your work and your assumptions. It is a valuable technique to catch mistakes, keep the team out of trouble, and allow team members to gain from others' experiences.

I have a confession to make—I am not perfect. Because of this, I make mistakes. In fact, I make a lot of them. My wife and kids, who have a front-row seat in observing my life, can certainly testify to this. In fact, my patient wife could probably write a whole book on my many, many mistakes. With this in mind, if NASA was expecting, over the course of my systems engineering duties, that I would never make a mistake in leading our mission development team, then we are all in *a lot* of trouble! That's why my mission teams always have a process where my work (and the work of everyone around me) is checked and double-checked because even the brightest and most well-intentioned people are fallible and make mistakes.

We have been told that no one likes someone looking over their shoulder while they are working on a task. There is a lot of truth to this sentiment. The very thought conjures up visions of a lack of confidence that the job will be done right and that a "checker" is needed to make sure a mistake is not made. Common wisdom suggests that most people would be insulted by such an action and would view it as signaling a serious lack of trust. On top of this, virtually no one would ever consider voluntarily asking someone to double-check their own work, as this might signal a lack of confidence in their own abilities.

While this may be a commonly accepted sentiment in the workplace, it is also a commonly accepted workplace falsehood that needs to be corrected. *Everyone* needs trusted people to double-check their work. The higher the stakes, the greater the need for a second set of eyes (or even a third set!) to make sure there are no mistakes. Not only do wise, experienced workers *not* get upset when someone checks or provides oversight over their work, typically the most experienced workers will seek this out on their own.

Most people have never heard of NASA's Mars Climate Orbiter mission. In fact, if you ask most folks working at NASA these days about this mission, you may get a blank look in response. However, if you were to instead ask them about "that NASA spacecraft that was lost due a mix-up between 'English' and metric units," virtually everyone would immediately recall that well-known NASA failure. That mission serves as a cautionary tale of a simple but legendary disconnect (see **"A Failure to Communicate"**) between the flight design team and the ground operations team, specifically in defining the units used to calculate the force used by the spacecraft's control thrusters. The spacecraft design team assumed the information would be in "English" units, while the ground operations system assumed the units would be in metric. As the spacecraft approached its aero-braking maneuver in the Martian atmosphere, this simple mismatch in units caused the spacecraft to miss the proper Martian entry trajectory and dip too low into the Martian atmosphere, likely breaking up and being destroyed due to atmospheric friction from the unplanned lower altitude. It was a heartbreaking loss of a mission just as it was reaching the finish line and getting ready to start its science mission. Dr. Edward Weiler, who at the time was the NASA Associate Administrator for Space Science, had this to say on the loss of the mission:

People sometimes make errors. The problem here was not the error; it was the failure of NASA's systems engineering, and the checks and balances in our processes to detect the error.[*]

Everyone makes mistakes. Part of the project leadership's role is to institute a process where these inevitable mistakes are recognized, caught, and corrected.

A mentor of mine is fond of reminding me that exploring space is exciting and challenging, but also very unforgiving. Over the course of a mission, thousands of good decisions can be undone by a single bad assumption, engineering flaw, or workmanship error. All it takes is one mistake to lose a mission, and, sadly, we don't get to choose in advance which mistake that will be, allowing us to head it off. It is worth noting that severe consequences due to uncaught errors are not unique to NASA—recalls, safety advisories, missed errors, and subsequent *mea culpas* occur across almost all industries and professions. As a result, we need to develop a multilayered defense to constantly check for and correct any inadvertent errors that could threaten mission success. This

---

[*] J. Oberg. December 1, 1999. "Why the Mars Probe Went Off Course," IEEE Spectrum, https://spectrum.ieee.org/why-the-mars-probe-went-off-course.

defense should include an assessment of various areas that could serve as "threats" to mission success, coupled with a set of intentional strategies designed to counter and mitigate these threats. A key aspect of that defense is a robust review process, otherwise known in layman's terms as "checking each other's work".

When we think of reviews, we often conjure up images of large conference rooms with formal presentations and formal review boards. This is certainly one aspect of the review process, one that is very important. NASA requires major independent reviews at the "gates" between every phase of a mission project lifecycle, and at every major mission milestone. The goal of these required reviews is to have external and independent teams "kick the tires" and evaluate a mission, its implementation approach, any issues the mission team may be facing and how they are addressing them, and the team's progress. The review team's purpose in doing this is to provide an independent check to make sure the project team hasn't missed anything that could disrupt or derail the project. This is the type of formal and structured review that people often picture when they think of "reviews".

These reviews are certainly valuable, but we need to consider "reviews" in the broader sense—as in having other people check our work, at every level of our work. We need to develop a habit of encouraging other skilled and knowledgeable people to look over our shoulders, at regular and reasonable points in mission development, not just at major reviews. If a team's work is only being reviewed at major formal milestones, there is a chance that something vital will slip through the cracks, perhaps resulting in an issue down the road, or even a mission anomaly or failure. We need to develop a culture (see **"Creating a Team Culture"**) that promotes regular reviews within our teams, encouraging qualified, trusted experts to look over our shoulders and check our work. Having other outside people review a project team's work also goes a long way in combating the risk of "groupthink" (see **"The Danger of No Dissent"**), where potential errors can be hidden from even well-meaning project teams.

Many project teams, recognizing the value of having others review their work, have developed a culture where there is a multilayered review approach. First, designers and technical teams will share their information within the team early in development at the grassroots level, encouraging others to look over their work to double-check their assumptions and results and see if there is anything that they have missed. This is a practice many projects have worked hard to instill in their development teams as a "first line of defense". Later, there may be a series of informal "tabletop" peer reviews with recognized "experts" within the organization. There should be little preparation for these reviews, reducing any "overhead" time required. Such reviews may consist of sitting around a conference room table and going over the design assumptions and products in an informal setting. The purpose is, again, to get another set of experienced eyes on the technical approach and implementation details to double-check the assumptions and the work. There may be multiple layers of these peer reviews, depending on the project and the nature of the mission.

Finally, there is the formal review process, such as the NASA review process identified previously. Typically, a good NASA review team will want to know if there were earlier, lower-level peer reviews, what the findings were, and how these findings were ultimately dispositioned and resolved.

These formal reviews take a lot of preparation and can seem like a waste of time, causing some to wonder if this distracts the team from the "real work". I believe nothing is further from the truth. The process of preparing for a review is, in itself, invaluable to a team. Time and time again, I have seen that a team's review preparation allows that team to stop and regroup, consolidating their latest work and examining it for self-consistency, and combining it into a cohesive product. Oftentimes, "holes" and inconsistencies are discovered through the consolidation process in review preparation, forcing the team to confront and resolve these disconnects. Finally, the final review product serves as a "snapshot in time" as to the status and issues that a project is facing. Many experienced senior engineers have shared that the primary value of a review actually ends when the first slide goes up, when the first presenter stands to begin talking. These senior engineers believe that a key value of a review is in the preparation process undertaken by the review team and the benefit that provides to the team itself.

It is important to emphasize that the fundamental principle here is to set up a process where experienced, trusted, and independent experts look over your team's work, with the goal of heading off issues you and your team may have missed. These reviewers are, in essence, partners in your project's efforts toward achieving mission success. However your team chooses to implement this process of getting another set of experienced eyes on your team's work, the important thing is to ensure that this independent "looking over your shoulder" actually occurs.

Guiding Principle: Everyone makes mistakes, which is why we all need someone looking over our shoulders and double-checking our work. Every leader should have a plan in place to ensure an independent review of their team's work on an ongoing basis, with the goal of catching and correcting any errors before they turn into major issues.

CHAPTER 20

Are You Better Off With Them or Without Them?

When I was very young, I was a voracious reader. I devoured everything I could get my hands on and often found myself with nothing new to read. As a result, I learned to read our daily newspaper each day, virtually cover to cover.

One of the things that I looked forward to reading each day, one of my guilty pleasures, was the advice column. Back then it was Ann Landers, doling out daily help to troubled souls who would turn to her for advice and wisdom, which she regularly dispensed. I was always amazed at the situations that people found themselves in (I was young back then and life was still relatively uncomplicated), yet Ann always seemed to have an apt response.

The most common issue that regularly arose dealt with marital problems, with people sharing their difficulties and asking Ann if they should leave their spouse (I always thought it odd that people would ask a *complete stranger* for advice on dissolving their marriage, but I digress). I always shook my head sadly when I would read these inquiries because I knew exactly what she would say. Ann's response was always the same for these types of questions and it *never* changed. Anyone who had read her column regularly would know that good 'ole Ann *always* responded the same way. She would always respond with the same question—"Ask yourself this question—are you better off *with them* or *without them?*" Once people determined for themselves the answer to this fundamental question, then they would know what to do.

I bring this up in order to address the next topic, one that bedevils everyone who has worked with or led a team of people—dealing with challenging and difficult people. I suspect that everyone has dealt with challenging people in the workplace. Entire books have been devoted to this topic as people search for answers and the "magic bullet" that will help them solve this ongoing issue.

Problem employees are the bane of the working world. It seems like every workplace has at least one problem employee that everyone just has to deal with. The conventional wisdom often seems to be that there is little to nothing that you can do with these people, that you just need to tolerate them as much as you can and consider them to be an unfortunate burden you are required to bear.

The problem with this type of fatalistic thinking is that it is simply wrong. Difficult employees are bad for the workplace, demotivate other employees, reduce productivity, and destroy morale. As with any challenge in the workplace, a good leader cannot just declare defeat and move on, but needs to develop a plan to deal with the challenge and address it. This is certainly not an easy problem to solve (which is why most employers simply give up), but one that must be addressed as part of creating a positive workplace environment.

First things first—if you have a seriously toxic or disruptive employee, you need to remove them from the rest of the team. Period. Either put them in another building or work area away from everyone else, or even remove them from your project. I know this sounds harsh, and I am a strong believer in second (and third) chances, but I have seen too many cases where a toxic and disruptive worker can destabilize an entire team and seriously impact the team culture (see **"Creating a Team Culture"**). Having shared this, let's move forward by assuming that the challenging employee does not rise to the level where such draconian actions are warranted.

I believe that, in many cases, there are practical reasons (and practical solutions) for what appears to be a troubled employee. In some cases, the employee is just the wrong fit for the job—perhaps their skill level or personality type is ill-suited for their current assignment. A practical response would be to work with them to find a position that is a better fit. I am a firm believer that there is a job where every person can thrive, it just may take some searching to discover it. Another possible solution may be that the individual needs more training or coaching to better understand the job and its demands. A patient leader or supervisor can make the difference in a troubled employee's life by helping them get over these hurdles and become more productive.

There are many similar cases to these, where employer strategies may help a struggling employee over the hump. A discerning leader needs to assess and determine if their worker may fall into one of these categories and what the best solution, if any, can move them forward.

Having briefly touched on these cases, let's focus our discussion on the "difficult" employee. You know the type—someone constantly pops up on your radar because of some challenging aspect of their behavior. I am assuming that this individual *must* have some valued skills, otherwise they wouldn't still be in your organization. Yet these types of workers often create disruption all around them and can be a challenge for any team leader.

I recall one instance where I had a skilled employee working for me who seemed to constantly create a disruptive environment. Not only did he threaten to distract the people working around him, but I was worried that the negative example he set, if unchecked, would start to spread throughout the team. I told a mentor of mine that I planned to have a talk with this individual, with the hope that it would set him straight and change his behavior. My mentor laughed, reminding me that this person was roughly 40 years old and had probably been this way most of his adult life. "How long of a 'talk' do you think it will take to change that type of deep-seated behavior?" he asked rhetorically. "Let's say you have a 'talk' with him every day—how many 'talks' do you think it will take before he changes who he is?" My mentor went on to share that it is very difficult to define and address "behavior", but instead my efforts should focus on "performance" and performance-related communication. These areas are more concrete and easier to define (as well as indirectly addressing behavior without making it the primary focus). My mentor went on to conclude that, instead of trying to "change" his attitude (which was unlikely), my role as a leader was instead to set clear parameters for performance and communication, make sure that these parameters were understood, and then monitor them regularly for compliance.

The idealist in me cringed at what I saw as a surrender of my principles of addressing poor behavior, but I eventually saw the practical sense in what was being shared. I decided to try to implement this approach. I sat this worker down, expressed my concerns, laid out guidelines on specific work-related performance and products that I expected, and made it clear that we would have regular follow-up meetings to assess progress. I was careful not to mention "attitude", which is hard to define and measure, but focused on performance and communication. Surprisingly, it was remarkably effective. What I found, however, was that this individual's personality was deeply ingrained—he could "toe the line" for a while, but then would eventually fall back into the same disruptive behavior which affected his performance and communication with others. When I saw this occurring, I would patiently meet with him again, remind him of our "plan", and performance and communication would improve—for a while—then the cycle would repeat. Frankly, it was a bit exhausting. But I was able to coax productive, skilled work out of this individual and was able to keep him—and his skills—on the team until the end of the project by using this technique.

This brings me back to good 'ole Ann Landers and her question—"Are you better off with them or without them?" I have had to ask myself this question many times on just about every project I have worked on, questioning myself about specific people over the course of a mission. Some people bring significant skills to the table, skills that are valuable to the team, but their personality or behavior comes at a cost. You need to decide if you are better off with them or without them. It may be that their skills are sufficiently unique and valuable such that you keep a challenging employee around because you need their skills. However, you will need to develop a strategy for ensuring that their "people drama" does not destabilize the rest of your team. Perhaps you will establish a recurring set of meetings as I described previously. Maybe you will seat them off to the side, by themselves, and minimize their interaction with the rest of the team as they undertake targeted assignments that are needed by your project development effort. Or maybe you will decide, after a time, that their skills, no matter how unique and valuable, are simply not worth the trouble, and you determine that you are better off without them and let them go. That is always a shame when it happens, but it does happen.

Please don't misunderstand the message being presented here. I am a strong advocate of mentoring and working with others. I have had many amazing mentors who have shaped me and my career (see **"The Value of a Mentor"**). Conversely, I have spent years and countless hours mentoring and building into younger engineers, which I have found immensely rewarding (see **"What, Me a Mentor?"**). I am a strong advocate of working to train and help employees grow whenever possible. I also believe that a good leader needs to be willing to go the extra mile to help out one of their workers when there is a need. Realistically, there are times when this simply doesn't work and, unfortunately, a leader has to consider other approaches and methods to address a challenging worker on their team.

There is a corollary lesson here that is important not to miss. If you are a difficult or challenging person yourself (see **"Wherever You Go, There You Are"**), you had better be *very* good at what you do. Otherwise, you may find yourself on the other side of this story. And even for incredibly talented people, there is a limit to when it is just not worth having you around and the team will decide, despite your skills, that they are better off without you.

Guiding Principle: When dealing with a challenging employee who has valued skills, an assessment needs to be made on whether the team is "better off with them or without them". If you choose to keep a challenging employee because of their valued skills, a strategy needs to be developed and implemented to keep them focused, productive, and minimize team disruptions.

CHAPTER 21

Are You an Impostor?

Richard was one of the best members of my team. He was smart and hardworking, always volunteering to take on some of the toughest assignments. He was a diligent worker, learned new things very quickly, and dove into every new challenge we faced. He was determined to learn and expand his knowledge base whenever possible in order to be better equipped for the challenging work we regularly faced. In addition, he was an excellent sounding board whenever I was struggling with a tough issue, and I found myself regularly at his office to seek his input on a wide variety of challenges that the team was facing. I felt extremely grateful to have him on my team.

But Richard had a secret, one that he did not tell anyone about. He was an impostor.

Actually, he really wasn't. But he thought he was. Richard quietly struggled with the feeling that he didn't measure up, that he didn't belong in his current position, and that he only got his current job due to an accident of fate or pure dumb luck. In a moment of honesty, he revealed to me that he lived with the fear that, one day, someone would realize that he didn't belong on our team, tap him on the shoulder, and he would be gone.

Of course, this was absolutely ridiculous. Richard was clearly one of the best members of my team and I didn't know what I would do without him. But he had this irrational fear that he didn't belong and would one day be found out.

I learned later that Richard was not alone. To my surprise, a large number of significant overachievers struggle with this same irrational concern. There is actually even a term for this, called "impostor syndrome". First described by psychologists Suzanne Imes and Pauline Rose Clance in the 1970s, the initial diagnosis focused on women in the workplace struggling with misplaced feelings of inadequacy. Since that time, studies have shown that this condition affects a surprising number of both men and women in the workplace and it is now getting much more attention.

Impostor syndrome is generally characterized as affecting high-performing individuals who are held in high respect and admiration in their workplaces. They often hold significant positions of recognition in their organizations or have excellent academic or workplace credentials. These individuals, despite their positions or the positive recognition they receive at work, feel that they are undeserving of their recognition. On the contrary, they often believe that they are not as intelligent or competent as others think they are. Instead, they believe that they ended up in the positions they currently hold due to luck or an oversight mistake, rather than their performance, and believe that they don't belong there. As a result, they often feel like frauds or "impostors", living in fear that others will eventually discover the "truth" about them and they will be exposed.

In most cases, these workers struggle silently with their hidden burden. In extreme cases, these feelings can be debilitating. Many workers who struggle with impostor syndrome, fearing being seen as a failure, resort to overworking themselves as the only way to meet expectations. On the outside, as a result, they seem like model employees. But, in severe cases, this negative view of themselves can be unhealthy and lead to all sorts of issues, including burnout.

A common misperception in the workplace is the thinking that our most productive and effective workers *know* that their work is outstanding, have a clear and positive view of themselves, and know their value to the organization. While this is true in many instances, I have learned over my many years in leading teams of highly talented individuals that this is not always the case. In fact, I have been surprised to discover that some of my most amazing workers actually struggle with feelings of self-doubt and wonder if they truly measure up. While not an out-and-out lie, this misperception hides the fact that some of our best and brightest workers struggle with feelings of doubt and inadequacy that does impact their performance and advancement in the workplace.

When Richard first confided in me that he worried that he would be "found out", I almost laughed out loud. Obviously, this was a ridiculous assertion, at least from my perspective, since Richard was without a doubt one of my best workers. Since that time, I have discovered that impostor syndrome is actually more common than I thought, especially among high-achieving workers (who I was surrounded by at NASA). By some estimates, 25 to 30 percent of high achievers regularly suffer from imposter syndrome. And around 80 percent of adults struggle with this at various points in their lives.

I've worked with a lot of people over my many years and I'm often surprised, as I get to know them better, to learn how many of these amazing workers actually feel insecure about their job performance and abilities. These are people who I would aggressively recruit for my team at the drop of a hat, yet they wonder if they are good enough. Ironically, I have also worked with a number of individuals with the opposite problem—an overabundance of self-assurance, oftentimes demonstrating overinflated confidence that is a bit misplaced and could use some toning down.

More and more organizations are recognizing that impostor syndrome is a real issue among our best and brightest. Understanding that many overachieving members of the team may struggle in this area makes this a source of concern, one worth discussing in order to better determine how to address it effectively. Not only is there a higher risk of burnout, but lingering self-doubt concerning their competence may mean that these valued workers avoid challenging assignments, promotions, or anything deemed "risky" out of fear of failure. This hampers a valuable employee from advancement and also hurts the team or organization. Organizations are always on the lookout for talented and promising employees to step into ever-increasing roles of responsibility and leadership, essentially allowing the organization to "grow from within". If an individual struggling with "impostor syndrome" is fearful that increasing responsibility may risk their "exposure", the organization potentially loses a valued worker who avoids advancing and filling vacancies in much-needed higher-level positions.

Studies show that the one key to addressing impostor syndrome is working to change a person's mindset and internal view about their own abilities. One of the top suggestions for accomplishing this is to talk about how they feel and help them to gain a proper view of themselves. It is especially important for these workers to create a support network at work, where they receive accurate and validating feedback from other people they respect. This is helpful for the employee and, in the process, helps to build a positive team culture within the organization. Another recommendation in dealing with these feelings is to talk to a trusted mentor (see **"The Value of a Mentor"**). Conversations like these with someone the worker trusts and looks up to can help those who struggle with these types of self-doubts understand that these feelings are normal, but also misplaced and irrational. Experts believe that this type of reinforcement from trusted mentors and leaders can go a long way in helping to adjust their thinking over time. This is where an astute leader comes in, who values their worker and the excellent work they provide to the team. This reinforcement can be as simple as taking the time to provide regular positive performance feedback from a trusted leader or supervisor and not just at an annual performance review. Good leaders will recognize that this is a positive and effective strategy for all employees, not just those who struggle with feelings of self-doubt. While taking the time to regularly recognize and praise all employees is a hallmark of an effective leader, employees needing reinforcement of their true value and worth may require this more frequently than others.

It is interesting that the strategies that have been shown to be effective in encouraging and helping those who struggle with imposter syndrome are the same strategies that effective leaders regularly use to provide feedback to their team members and create a healthy work environment. Remembering to implement these strategies across the entire team is a good practice and is an excellent reminder to encourage people and highlight their work.

Guiding Principle: A significant subset of high-performing individuals may struggle with "impostor syndrome", a false narrative downplaying their contributions and value to the organization. This false self-image makes them more prone to negative

events such as burnout and may cause them to intentionally limit their own development. An observant leader will employ strategies to regularly provide positive feedback to help these employees see their true worth to the team. As a bonus, when widely employed across the team, these strategies will also serve to encourage and validate the entire team and reinforce a positive team culture.

CHAPTER 22

The Big Red Line

One of the themes of this book is the lies and mistruths that we are told in the workplace and the need to dispel and debunk them. Most of the time, these falsehoods come masquerading as something else, which often makes them hard to spot. However, this is not always the case. Sometimes, the lies are much more direct.

For example, I vividly remember the day when I was asked to lie at work.

I consider myself to be an ethical person. I think most people probably see themselves in the same light. Over the years, I have often thought through how I would respond if I was asked to do something unethical at work. I had rehearsed it out in my head many times, how I would stand firm and say "No!", letting everyone know that my integrity wasn't for sale at any price. I was ready.

But when that day came, it was not as I had imagined it would be at all. I realized later that challenges to your integrity often do not come in a full-frontal assault, they often come sideways, in ways that are not immediately obvious. When I was asked to lie at work, it was in a similar fashion, starting with a simple "bending" of inconvenient truths. It was all so reasonable that, at first, it was hard to tell. Rarely does someone come right out and say "I want you to do something unethical" or "I want you to lie." The line is rarely that clear-cut. Instead, it starts as small steps that seem innocuous. Someone asks you to give a more positive report than is merited, to "bend" some data to make test results look more positive, to present a more "optimistic" take on something than what the actual truth is, or perhaps even to "look the other way" on something that could be negatively perceived—almost never is it a clear-cut falsehood that would immediately raise the alarm. At first, it may almost seem reasonable. Then one day, you realize that your conscience is bothering you and you have to decide what to do.

I freely admit it, I'm a bit old-fashioned. While I am certainly not perfect, I believe in honesty and integrity, and that your word should count for something. I think these values help create a good workplace culture of trust and integrity, and their absence creates a toxic and unhealthy workplace culture. In addition, I think truth is important not only in maintaining integrity in the workplace—but is also a good engineering practice, since our work depends on truth and presenting the facts as plainly as possible.

I recently watched an excellent TV series entitled, *The Dropout*. It told the true story of Elizabeth Holmes, who founded the company Theranos, which was going to revolutionize the blood-analyzing industry. She became the darling of Silicon Valley with her concept of blood analyzing using only a drop of blood instead of the multiple vials that were the current industry practice. Her startup raised hundreds of millions of dollars in investor funding and the company valuation was $10 billion at its peak, all based on the promise of her revolutionary approach. There was just one problem—the Theranos prototype blood analyzers did not work reliably. There is a scene in the TV series that shows the day that she crossed the line. There was an investor demo planned for the next day, and the blood analysis machine was still working unreliably. After staying up all night trying unsuccessfully to get the machine to work, she and her team decided to fudge the results to pass the demo, to lie. They told themselves that this was just a stopgap measure until they could get the machine working properly. They told themselves that this was all part of the Silicon Valley startup mentality, where you "fake it till you make it", that all successful startups do the same thing. So, they lied. After the first lie, more lies were required to prop up the first one. Eventually, the whole company became based on the continuation of that very first lie. For those who follow the news, you know the rest of the story. Eventually, the whole house of cards fell down. It was revealed that the new approach that they promised didn't actually work. The company, once valued in the billions, became worthless. Investors lost all their money, hundreds of millions of dollars worth. Elizabeth Holmes went on trial for fraud, was found guilty, and went to jail. And it all started with one little lie which, to her, seemed like a simple bending of the truth to get past a problem that day.

I've informally asked my friends and co-workers to see if any of them have ever been asked to lie in their jobs. Some have suggested that, at some point in their careers, they have felt pressured to bend the truth to an uncomfortable degree to fit the narrative that others wanted to present. Surprisingly, a few have told me that they were directly asked to lie. All of them felt uncomfortable and, once they realized what was going on, many said no.

That's what happened to me. Once I fully understood that I was being asked to lie, I emphatically said no. The person who was trying to push me in that direction immediately backtracked, denying there was anything improper with what they were asking me to do. But they also didn't ask me again, almost as if they realized that they had been caught.

The problem with lies is that they tend to build on one another. Just like Elizabeth Holmes and Theranos, she and her team likely thought that all they needed was one tiny white lie, just a small stretching of the truth, allowing them to get past a critical demo. Then another lie was needed to back up the first one, and so on, and so on. There are moral reasons to tell the truth (I won't go into those, I believe that they are self-evident), but there are also practical ones as well. Frankly, my memory is simply not good enough to keep track of a bunch of lies, and telling the truth is so much easier. There's the technical side, where technical results built on lies or dishonest reporting create a precarious foundation to build upon and move forward. Eventually, the risk grows that subsequent technical results will cause those lies to be discovered (as in the case of Elizabeth Holmes and Theranos). Then there's the matter of your reputation. Once you get labeled as a dishonest person at work, no one will *ever* fully trust you again. That label will follow you for the rest of your career. As an example, I recall an instance, early in my career, when my supervisor seriously savaged another co-worker's reputation in a private conversation with me. Surprised, I asked where this negative attitude toward this co-worker originated. My supervisor revealed that he had previously caught this co-worker telling a lie in a major presentation to a review team. When asked a question by the review team that he didn't know the answer to, this co-worker had a choice. Instead of admitting he didn't know and offering to check on the answer and get back to the review team, he gave a very convincing lie instead, one that no one saw through except my supervisor. "After that," my supervisor told me, "I *never* trusted him again. He simply lies too well."

It certainly is not lost on me that there may be consequences for refusing to go along with a lie or bending the truth. Typically, when someone asks you to be deceptive or unethical, there is a power imbalance involved, with the person asking you to lie being in a position above you. That can be uncomfortable and, in some cases, may be career-limiting. That's why you need to decide in advance how you will respond, and realize that an organization that encourages deception may not be an organization you want to be part of in the long term. I firmly believe that no job is worth being pressured to compromise your core values. If someone is asking you to do just that, it doesn't sound like that job is a good fit for you and it might be time to start looking for a new job.

You'll notice that, unlike every other chapter in this book, I'm not giving any further details to this story and how this encouragement for me to lie unfolded. No names, dates, or other identifying details. That is by design, because the details don't matter and I'm not trying to get anyone in trouble. I'm just providing this as a warning that challenges to your ethics may come, and, when they do, they may not come with a lot of obvious warning signs. Challenges to your integrity may come sideways, like they did for me, and catch you by surprise. They may even masquerade as a simple bending of the truth, that "everyone does it", that the organization is just trying to buy time until favorable results catch up to these promises later on, that just a little more time is needed. I am highlighting this as an encouragement to be ready and resist those excuses and hold on to your ethics and your integrity before crossing that line and going down an unpleasant path.

Guiding Principle: You may face an instance where you will be asked to bend the truth for work or to do something you feel is unethical or goes against your value system. This request is often not straightforward and is likely to be much more nuanced than you expect. You should determine in advance how you will respond so you will be ready if it occurs.

CHAPTER 23

Avoiding Blind Spots

One of the common lies in the workplace is that individuals can advance more rapidly in an organization by being a "yes man"—that is, being an individual who agrees with everything their leader says or does. Typically, this is done to ingratiate themselves with those in leadership, often out of a desire for job security and advancement. Sometimes, being overly agreeable in this fashion is simply done to avoid uncomfortable situations or conflicts at work.

Some misguided leaders may actually like this type of individual, as it makes them feel smart and important. Another related workplace falsehood is that having people like this working underneath you can actually provide a self-esteem boost and make you a better and more confident leader. The reality is that these people are dangerous, preventing those in leadership from clearly examining themselves, exercising necessary critical thinking, and seeing their "blind spots".

As a result of these concerns, I always worked to surround myself with people who would honestly (and, hopefully, respectfully) tell me the truth, whether I liked it or not. One of these invaluable people was Toby.

Toby had worked alongside me for many years at Goddard and I had learned to rely on him quite heavily in many areas of my work. He was smart, had an insatiable desire to learn, and was curious about everything. As a result, he would make it his mission to get to the bottom of every problem, learn about every new technology we were planning to fly, and make a point to be well-educated on every potential issue that could threaten us. He was an invaluable asset to me and was one of my key "go-to" guys when I ran into a seemingly unsolvable problem and needed help.

He was also a pain in the neck.

Toby always told it exactly the way it was, often poking hornets' nests in the process. He enjoyed tweaking people whenever possible, it seemed. He was also one of the most perceptive people I've ever worked with and had astute powers of observation. As a result, Toby could usually read a room or determine a person's character or work ethic long before I could. And he *always* told the truth, typically with his characteristic bluntness and a mischievous bent. And that was where he was invaluable to me. I could always count on Toby telling me the unvarnished truth, whether I liked it or not. My ego was never going to get very big around him, because he would always let me know exactly where I was slipping or made a mistake (and, on rare occasions, when I did well). It was never mean-spirited, just blunt and to the point. While I would certainly rather someone fawn over me and tell me how great I was, I found his insights and observations to be extremely valuable, and they helped to keep me well-grounded and self-aware. I once told him, "Toby, you're really a pain in the neck at times, but you're always honest. Please don't stop being honest, because then you'll just be a pain in the neck." Surprisingly, he always seemed pleased by comments like those.

There is tremendous value in having people like Toby at your side. While they can be annoying at times, everyone needs someone around them who "tells it like it is". All of us have blind spots, where we don't see ourselves very clearly. Just like the blind spots that exist in our vehicle field-of-view when driving, ignoring what is lurking in our personal blind spots can lead to unintended accidents. That's why all of us need trusted allies who tell us the truth and point out areas of needed growth and improvement, even when it hurts or is uncomfortable to hear.

Over my lengthy career, I have worked with a great number of managers and technical leaders. Some of them were amazing leaders who I respected immensely, and who possessed exceptional qualities that I admired and still work hard to emulate. Sadly, I have also worked under some very poor managers and leaders. A few of them were truly horrendous, to the point that I legitimately wondered how they got their jobs and why they were not removed. As I observed both types of leaders, I noticed one significant thing that differentiated these two groups of people. The primary difference I could see between good and poor leaders was whether or not they surrounded themselves with trusted people who were willing and able to give them honest feedback and speak the truth to them.

In the case of the leaders that I admired, they surrounded themselves with trusted, experienced people who they sought out for advice and from whom they were willing to accept input. Their leadership approach was characterized by their openness to feedback. This openness extended to the working level employees as well. One senior leader who I admired immensely would regularly walk the hallways of the engineering department, stopping employees in the hall to chat, and regularly stopping by labs and spacecraft testing facilities. It was clear to me that he was always very intentional about keeping his pulse on how employees felt and any questions or concerns they had. It was senior leaders like these that, even when I was a junior employee, I would feel the freedom to share my thoughts and concerns with, even though they were multiple levels up the management chain. I was often surprised when these same leaders would follow up with me later, demonstrating that they had heard and considered what I had shared. It was readily apparent that these leaders went out of their way to solicit inputs from others in order to get a clear view of how the organization was working (or wasn't working) as well as personal feedback on how they were doing as leaders. One thing these types of leaders all had in common was their habit of surrounding themselves with people who were willing and able to speak the truth to them.

For the leaders I didn't admire or respect, the exact opposite was true. From what I could see, one thing these poor (in my opinion) leaders all had in common is that they did *not* surround themselves with people who could give them honest input. In fact, from my outsider's perspective, it appeared that the opposite was true. These leaders were insulated from any outside inputs and were disconnected from the people who worked underneath them in their organization. This prevented them from receiving any feedback about their poor leadership and the actual problems and dysfunction in their organization. From my observations, the worse the leader, the more insulated they were from input from those around them. As a result, the avenues for them to receive professional feedback were limited, and there did not seem to be anyone in place who was willing or able to speak the truth to them. Rather than engaging people at the working level, the people in their organization were often cowed into silence and, in the worst cases, afraid to speak up for fear of retribution. There was often a culture of fear or intimidation that prevented people from speaking up.

Again, a common thread that seemed to connect these widely divergent leadership types was the degree to which they surrounded themselves with individuals who could provide honest feedback, either from trusted lieutenants or even from those at the working level. I have often wondered about the "chicken and the egg" aspect of this connection—were they good/bad leaders because they did/didn't have people around them who honestly told them the truth, or did they allow/reject people around them who spoke the truth because they were good/bad leaders? I have my personal suspicions, but the important point is how essential it is for all leaders to surround themselves with people who can provide honest input on their performance and other issues associated with their work. Those leaders who allow and even solicit this type of input will always tend to be better and more productive. Conversely, those who do not allow this type of input run the risk of becoming a cautionary tale of poor leadership.

It is important to note that the need for honest feedback is not just a good practice for upper-level management and senior technical leaders but is applicable to all workers at every level. In fact, the habits that are cultivated early in a career often carry through as one rises up through the ranks. With this in mind, a good set of diagnostic questions for every leader (and every worker) to ask themselves are the following: Who do *you* have around you who speaks truth to you, even when it hurts? Do you give these individuals permission to tell you the truth, even if they disagree with you? If you have someone who comes to mind in response to these questions, ask yourself this: when was the last time this individual came up to you and provided some negative or uncomfortable feedback? If it hasn't been recently, either you are doing everything perfectly (which is unlikely) or perhaps you don't have the trusted and experienced feedback source that you thought you did and need to re-evaluate or make an effort to actively solicit input.

Guiding Principle: We all have blind spots. Good leaders surround themselves with trusted and experienced people who are willing to give them honest feedback and to (respectfully) challenge them and hold them accountable. In addition, these leaders will also actively solicit feedback to remain grounded and avoid "blind spots". Poor leaders create an environment where this type of feedback does not occur and is even actively discouraged.

CHAPTER 24

The Value of Worry

My most valued mentor is Mike, who I met early in my NASA career and has taught me most of what I know (which is still substantially less than what he knows). In addition to being the best systems engineer I have ever worked with, he is probably one of the nicest guys I have ever met as well, a true gentleman.

However, when he is worried about a technical issue on a project, he becomes a different person. He is relentless. You can tell when Mike is concerned about a problem because he is like a dog with a bone—he is singularly focused, a man on the hunt. He will not let anything (or anyone) get in his way until he convinces himself that his worry is unfounded or it is resolved. Sometimes, he can be unintentionally brusque or rub people the wrong way while he is engaged in chasing down a problem. Once the potential problem is resolved, then he goes back to his normal kind and friendly self.

I asked Mike about this once, why he becomes so intensely focused when he is worried about a potential technical issue. He told me that he worries that he may be the last "gate" in solving a problem, the final defense between a potential problem and launch day. He went on to share that he lives with the worry that, if he doesn't chase down and catch a potential problem, there is a chance it could slip through and become a serious issue in orbit. And it is things like that, he concluded, that worry him and keep him up at night.

I admire Mike's intense sense of ownership. I know many other excellent systems engineers and technical workers who exhibit the same qualities. I've worked hard in my own NASA career to emulate these characteristics and I'm sure I have been just as annoying in chasing down a potential problem as Mike has been. In the process, I have learned something important.

I have learned, contrary to popular belief, that worry can be good. To be honest, I'm not sure that I would want someone on my team who doesn't worry about things.

Worry gets a bad rap these days. Experts tell us that worry can lead to anxiety, depression, and all sorts of health issues. We're encouraged to "don't worry, be happy." I understand and agree with all of this.

But worry is a vital component to good engineering and, frankly, to life. Appropriate worry helps us to search for and identify small concerns on the distant horizon, allowing them to be addressed before they become huge disasters deposited on our doorstep, threatening to overwhelm us. A life devoid of worry can be risky, leading to missing emerging issues until they become full-fledged problems that can have significant consequences.

Worry is a double-edged sword, to be sure. People who don't worry may be ignoring real concerns. But worry can also paralyze us. We likely all know people who have allowed worry to take over and control every aspect of their lives. The same thing can happen in a workplace environment, where a member of the team becomes inundated with all the things that could go wrong and becomes overwhelmed, unable to sort through them effectively to determine which should be prioritized. Managing and assessing worry is a vital part of life. The challenge before us is how to make sure that "worry" is a constructive force in our lives that helps us to spot emerging problems before they grow out of control, but also to prevent worry from ruining our lives. There are practical ways to manage worry to ensure that we deal with real issues but don't allow it to consume us.

One of the simplest ways I classify worry when I explain it to my co-workers and friends is to group worry into two major categories: "good" worry and "bad" worry.

"Good" worry essentially describes potential areas of concern over which an individual has some degree of control. Being worried about something in this category means that there are some concrete steps, either big or small, that an individual can consider and choose to take, potentially mitigating the concern they are worried about. For example, if I am worried about my car battery going dead on a cold day at work, one action I could take would be to throw some jumper cables in the back of my car and hope someone is there who can help me jumpstart my dead battery if it were to actually happen. Or, even better, I can buy a handheld portable car jump starter, removing the need for assistance or outside help. "Good worry" deals with concerns where there is a realistic chance of the event happening and there are reasonable things within your control that you can do to mitgate it, concrete steps that you can take to address the event if it were to occur.

"Bad" worry, on the other hand, deals with things that are typically out of your control. In addition, besides being out of your control and relatively unlikely to happen, there's not that much that you could practically do to mitigate these potential events. For example, if you are worried about the potential for nuclear war, I would classify this as "bad worry". There's probably nothing you can do to avoid or mitigate this, you're better off focusing on things that are more under your control.

Even with "good worry", you can get overwhelmed by the sheer number of potential issues that could be heading your way. There needs to be some effort to filter the possible worries and categorize them from the most likely to the least likely. This allows the most likely potential problems to be dealt with first, with the less likely ones to remain on the back burner.

Engineers have developed their own method of classifying and breaking down their potential concerns in a way that allows a team to clearly assess and deal with them. Every NASA project has a clearly defined risk process that is used to document potential threats to the mission. Each potential threat is documented as a project risk and is assigned a likelihood (i.e., what are the chances that this problem could occur?) and a consequence (i.e., if this problem actually did occur, how bad would the impact be to the project?). The risk process is covered elsewhere (see **"Risky Business"**), but it is important to note that NASA engineers don't just worry about things, they have a clear process to document their worries into a system that allows them to address and mitigate them (putting them in the "good worry" category).

As we mentioned elsewhere, exploring space is exciting and challenging, but also very unforgiving (see **"Someone Looking Over**

Your Shoulder"). In the cutting-edge business of spaceflight development, if an engineer or leader is NOT concerned about the things that could go wrong and cause a mission to fail, it likely means that individual isn't paying close enough attention. There is a standard question that I have found is typically asked at every review, at the end of each presentation, after all other questions have been asked. A reviewer will ask the presenter in relation to their technical discipline area, "What keeps you up at night?" A good translation of that question would be, "What are you worried about?" A good engineer typically has a ready answer to that question, revealing that they are always worried about what could go wrong. I would be concerned about any engineer who isn't.

Guiding Principle: Worry can serve as a warning sign that there may be legitimate areas of concern that need to be addressed. A good team will collect and assess these worries in a logical fashion, classifying and breaking down any potential concerns in a manner that allows the team to clearly evaluate and mitigate them. Ignoring worries may expose a team to greater problems down the road since neglected concerns could grow into major problems.

CHAPTER 25

Risky Business

Although they often make it look easy, NASA missions are often daring and extremely challenging. Occasionally, NASA will pull aside the curtain and let the public see how risky a mission really is. While there are many examples of this, an excellent one to highlight is the landing of the *Curiosity* rover on the surface of Mars. There is an excellent video on YouTube entitled, "7 Minutes of Terror: The Challenges of Getting to Mars." If you haven't seen it, you need to put down this book right now and watch it.

This video, released before the landing, shows how insanely hard the Mars landing was—and how many things had to work perfectly to pull it off. It is mind-boggling. I often wondered if NASA released this video before the landing as a way to prepare the public for the possibility that this daring event would fail and the approximately two billion dollar rover would be lost. As I viewed this video, I couldn't believe how risky this landing sequence looked. Even one of the engineers, at the beginning of the video, states, "When people look at it, it looks crazy. That's a very natural thing. Sometimes when we look at it, it seems crazy."

Like many NASA missions, it is clear that there were a myriad of things that all had to work just perfectly for the rover landing to be successful. But I can assure you that the NASA engineering team didn't just cross their fingers and hope that everything would work fine. As the engineer says at the beginning of the video, "It seems crazy." But he goes on to say, "It is the result of reasoned engineering thought." Not luck, not hope, not wishful thinking.

In my own experience, building state-of-the-art spacecraft and launching them into space is inherently risky business. NASA engineers and their partners are constantly pushing the envelope to use state-of-the-art technology and processes to squeeze out the latest science in order to better help us understand our amazing universe. Most of the time, they succeed and accomplish amazing things. Sometimes, they fail. But it is almost always a risky business. Part of the NASA engineers' job is to quantify that risk so that the Agency goes into every mission with their eyes open and not just blindly hoping that everything works. As a mentor of mine once told me, we never launch a mission on "hope".

One of the ways that engineers manage and assess all the things that they worry could go wrong (and there are *a lot* of these things to worry about over the course of a mission) is by employing a risk process. The risk process is what keeps the engineering team from simply worrying and hoping that everything just goes well. Every worry is assessed to determine if it can be distilled into a potential problem that could negatively impact the mission. If so, it is documented as a risk.

One of the common falsehoods that I have run into in the workplace deals with identifying and documenting risks. To be blunt, most people don't want to do it. They are aware that there are risks and they want to keep an eye on them, but they are hesitant to formally document potential problems for fear that their project will look overly "risky" and invite undue scrutiny (which nobody wants, right?). Better to quietly keep track of any potential risks on your own and deal with them "in-house". The problem with this short-sighted approach is that keeping risks "quiet" removes the opportunity for additional sets of eyes to examine the risks, help evaluate them, and assist in helping to mitigate and close them out. A robust and formal risk process, while opening up a team to additional scrutiny, is one of the best ways to understand and mitigate potential problems and increase the chances of mission success, whether you work for NASA or any other workplace.

The goal of the risk process is to document potential problems, clearly understand them, and put a plan in place to address and mitigate them by reducing their potential likelihood or impact. Every risk starts by clearly documenting the potential problem and what the unfavorable outcome could be. The risk is then assigned a "likelihood" (i.e., what are the chances of this actually happening?) and a "consequence" (i.e., if this did actually occur, what would the effect be?). This combination of likelihood and consequence allows the project team to rank risks in order of importance. Finally, suggested mitigation steps (i.e., what are concrete steps that can be done to diminish or eliminate the negative outcome?) are documented as well. The goal of this entire process is to better understand all the potential threats to the mission, as well as come up with ways to eliminate these threats.

Every engineer worries (at least, they should, in my opinion). Unresolved worry, however, can overwhelm and paralyze even the most experienced and well-grounded engineer (see **"The Value of Worry"**). Conversely, legitimate concerns can be discarded prematurely, which could result in them growing into even bigger problems down the road. The risk process is a practical method to take these worries and bring them to the mission team. The mission team can then carefully assess them to see if they are grounded in a specific potential problem that is likely to impact the mission. If the team agrees that this is the case, then a specific risk is documented, along with an assessment and a plan to mitigate that risk. Using this approach, vague worries are carefully assessed and either promoted to a risk or discarded. This allows the team to focus on the concrete issues that they need to address to ensure mission success and to track them to ensure that they don't fall through the cracks.

A robust risk process is one of the best ways for the project team to clearly communicate among themselves what they are truly worried about (see **"A Failure to Communicate"**), making sure nothing is missed or swept under the rug, and helping to ensure that potential problems are addressed. The risk process is sometimes the last refuge of the concerned engineer. On the one hand, an engineer may be unduly worried about specific areas, with this worry threatening to defocus them from the big picture and other legitimate concerns. The risk process provides an opportunity to get a project-level review of such items and assist the engineer in determining if their concerns are valid or overblown. On the other hand, it may be the last chance for a concerned individual who feels that they have a legitimate concern that, for whatever reason, is not getting traction with the project. Documenting these concerns as a proposed risk helps to address both of these cases and brings potential issues up to the larger team for review. I have found that, once I understood and learned to use it properly, the risk process was an extremely valuable tool in my systems engineering toolbox.

We mentioned earlier that documenting project risks and laying them out for everyone to see may be good for your team, but it can open you up to undue attention and criticism from others. Some believe that a large number of documented risks may identify a project as "risky" and garner unwanted negative attention and oversight. I have never agreed with this, firmly believing instead that the more legitimate risks that are recorded and tracked, the more project management is aware of potential problems that require extra attention. My experience is that a robust and well-documented risk program will convince even the most hardened reviewers and outside observers that the project team has their eyes wide open and clearly understands the challenges in front of them.

One final thought—much of the discussion in this chapter has been from an engineering perspective and promotes using some sort of formal risk documentation system (I can't help it, that's the background I come from and what I'm familiar with). However, the value in identifying, documenting, and tracking potential problems that your organization might be facing is universal, no matter what line of work you are in. Doing this will allow you to keep an eye on potential problem areas to prevent them from blowing up and causing your organization a headache. Following some sort of process to identify, track, and alleviate potential problems will be of tremendous value to your organization, whatever line of work you are in.

Guiding Principle: Every team faces a variety of potential problems that can threaten their success. Clearly documenting these potential problems in a risk system is an excellent threat reduction approach. A good risk system is one that allows potential problems to be identified, documented, clearly understood, ranked, tracked, and mitigated. Implementing this type of approach is the best way to decrease the chances that potential problems will seriously impact the path forward.

CHAPTER 26

Breaking the Rules

A common phase in the workplace is the axiom *"Rules are made to be broken"*. Honestly, I hate this saying, almost as much as I hate the saying *"It's easier to ask for forgiveness than it is to ask for permission."* While I wouldn't necessarily call them workplace lies, both imply a casual disregard for rules, authority, and valued lessons that have been passed down in the workplace.

If you haven't figured it out yet, truth be told, I am by nature a rule follower. I always have been, and I believe it is deeply embedded in my DNA. I believe that most rules are in place for our good, to keep us safe and protected. Most of the people who know me well have figured out that I am wired this way. I suspect that's why my project team was so surprised when I told them to ignore one of Goddard's official design rules in one of our mission design concepts.

As a deeply ingrained rule follower, I typically don't ignore rules or other well-established practices without careful consideration. However, as every good leader knows, there may be times when rules need to be bent or discarded. Knowing when and how to follow or discard a given rule is the key, and doing so properly can mean the difference between an innovative success and a crashing failure. In fact, the quote about *"rules are made to be broken"* was made by General Douglas MacArthur and is actually only part of what he really said. His full quote is *"Rules are mostly made to be broken and are too often for the lazy to hide behind."* I believe the point that General MacArthur was trying to get across was that while rules may be in place for a reason, it is important to understand the purpose behind those reasons and whether they apply to a given situation rather than simply blindly following them. Blindly following rules without understanding why they are there is in no one's best interests.

This important discussion takes us back to why we have rules, what they are for, why they should be followed, and, most importantly, why they shouldn't be followed blindly. To understand this, let's examine where most good rules originate—from people making mistakes.

Many people incorrectly assume that very smart people don't make mistakes. I can assure you that this is *not* true. Smart people actually make a lot of mistakes, perhaps more than most. Over the years, NASA engineers have made lots and lots of mistakes. That's what happens when you are doing things that no one else has done before and are constantly pushing the boundaries of what is known and achievable. These "mistake makers" were not dummies either, they were some of the smartest people you can imagine. However, the big difference between these engineers and most people is that they *learn* from their mistakes. Goddard has a large repository of "best practice" rules that are based on this trial-and-error process, where smart people made a lot of mistakes and, in the process, learned a lot and developed some smart practices to avoid these kinds of mistakes in the future. These "best practices" are often bundled up into a set of formal "rules" for others to understand and follow and often include design guidelines and margins that serve as "guardrails" to keep other engineers out of trouble and prevent them from repeating the mistakes of the past. Other engineers and technical leaders would be wise to understand and heed these rules, and anyone who ignores them does so at their own peril.

These Goddard rules provide excellent guidance on practices that you should follow and things you should not do. In general, if you follow them, you will stay out of trouble. But they are not absolutes. As with all things, there are exceptions. For every documented "rule", the documentation includes the principle behind it that is the basis of the rule and why it exists. By understanding the intent behind the rule and what a specific rule is designed to protect you from, one may discover instances where it does not fully apply—and where exceptions may exist.

Sometimes understanding the reason for the rule or the intent behind it can be very illuminating and can help to understand if a particular rule is actually applicable to a given situation or not. I often share a simple example that illustrates this when I present this topic in classes to younger engineers. On an earlier mission, I told them, we had a hard requirement about taking closeout photos of flight boards and electronics. After the flight units were closed up and fully assembled, there are sometimes questions on the contents of the flight units and how they were manufactured, or an anomaly may crop up that needs investigation. In those cases, the closeout photos taken *before* the units were fully assembled could be carefully examined for clues instead of forcing the team to incur risk and schedule delays by reopening the flight unit for a visual examination. These photos have proven to be very helpful in determining if there were any workmanship errors that had been missed earlier. The hard requirement in question was the following: closeout photos could only be taken with traditional analog (film) cameras and *not* with digital cameras. I then asked the class to explain to me why this specific requirement was in place. The class struggled for a long time and actually came up with a few very creative (but ultimately incorrect) reasons for this requirement. Finally, I told them the reason this requirement had been enacted. At the time (around 1999–2001), digital cameras did not have the sufficient resolution required for high-fidelity closeout photo evaluation, making them unsuitable for this purpose. Only analog cameras had the sufficient resolution that was needed to see fine details on circuit card assemblies populated with tiny electronic components. At the time the requirement was established, it was easier to simply list a requirement rather than state the underlying principle that "all photos of flight hardware should have the necessary resolution to evaluate the hardware." Since that time, digital photo technology has progressed to the point that digital cameras have became equal or superior to analog cameras, rendering this requirement obsolete. However, this requirement could be discarded only *if* the intent behind the requirement was understood—otherwise, it might, as obsolete as it was, remain in place. I closed by telling the class that it is *always* important to know *why* a rule is in place and what the rule is guarding against. Understanding the intent allows a more educated assessment of the requirement, possibly enabling pushback against a rule rather than blindly accepting it.

In the case of our design team (my rule-breaking activity from the beginning of this chapter), they were struggling with how to implement a challenging aspect of our mission design and kept bumping into one of these Goddard rules, which was clearly intended to keep us out of trouble. We kept looking for alternate solutions but came up empty time and time again. I finally asked them, "What if there were no Goddard design rules and you just had to come up with a reliable, safe and effective design. What would be the right thing to do?" Their response was immediate and unanimous. If it wasn't for that pesky rule, our chosen approach was easily the correct path forward and would result in a clever and reliable design implementation. In fact, our approach, while not meeting the "letter" of the rule, was one that the team all felt would meet the underlying intent behind the rule.

With this in mind, I told them to ignore the rule and work on further developing this design approach. When I saw their shocked looks, I told them that we weren't actually *ignoring* the rule, we had just come to the conclusion that we had found an approach that met the *underlying intent*. As a result, we were still avoiding the danger that the rule was intended to protect us from. However, because we were proposing that our team deviate from a standard Goddard practice, we would need to submit a waiver for our approach, which meant that other qualified (yet independent) experts would evaluate our proposed plan to ensure that we were not making a well-intentioned mistake.

It is important to note that ignoring any established rule or requirement should not be done casually. There is an old saying that states "Do not remove a fence until you know why it was put up in the first place." The Goddard design rules have checks and balances in place to prevent overeager engineers from inadvertently making this kind of mistake. The Goddard rules system is set up so that any proposed waiver (like ours) is required to be reviewed and approved by the "rule holder" (the technical expert behind the rule in question). This process is designed to ensure that any waiver is carefully reviewed (see **"Someone Looking Over Your Shoulder"**) and any unanticipated results are considered by an independent source. It's possible that some design teams may request waivers without fully considering all the risks of circumventing a particular rule, opening their project up to undue risk. These types of poorly formulated waivers are typically denied and those teams are sent back to the drawing board to come up with another solution to their problem. But sometimes a smart, insightful team understands the reason for the rule and makes a convincing argument that their approach meets the *intent* of the rule (but perhaps not the "letter" of the rule) and satisfies the rationale on why the rule was originally put in place. Those waivers are carefully reviewed and, if there is agreement among the technical experts, are approved. In addition to this initial review and approval, any approved waivers of this type are also presented at every major project lifecycle review, allowing an independent review team to verify there were not any missteps.

Rene Descartes, the famous mathematician and philosopher, was known for saying "Each problem that I solved became a rule, which served afterwards to solve other problems." Most rules exist for a reason, both in engineering and in life. They are generally based on hard-won lessons and reflect well-established principles to keep from repeating past mistakes. Individuals who ignore these well-established rules do so at their own peril. However, there are exceptions to every rule, and these exceptions need to be considered on a case-by-case basis. They should not be considered casually, and teams should *always keep in mind what the driving principle behind the rule was in order to see if it is still applicable.* Always be willing to *respectfully* push back against a rule or requirement to see if it is applicable or relevant to your specific case. Rules should never be accepted blindly without verifying their applicability to your situation. By doing due diligence in this manner, your team may unexpectedly find solutions or a path forward that they might have otherwise missed.

Guiding Principle: Most rules and requirements exist for a reason and we ignore them at our own peril. However, always be willing to respectfully push back against a rule or requirement to understand the intent and the "reason why", ensuring that the underlying purpose behind the rule is understood and applicable. In some cases, there may be alternate approaches that will allow the original intent of the rule to be satisfied in another manner.

CHAPTER 27

Recovering From Failure

Almost everyone has an instance at work where they have made a mistake. There are two commonly believed falsehoods associated with mistakes in the workplace—either believing that good people *never* make mistakes (untrue) or that a *big* mistake can somehow disqualify you from recovering and succeeding in future endeavors (also untrue). Some of these mistakes we make can be really, really big, so big that they can make us feel humiliated and can seem as if they are almost unrecoverable. Often, when we make a mistake and feel humiliated, our natural instinct is to run away and hide out of embarrassment, especially if the failure is due at least in part to our actions (or lack of action). How we recover once we've been knocked down tells a lot about who we are and what we're made of.

One of my most humiliating mistakes occurred early in my career at NASA. I was the lead engineer of a team developing a set of flight avionics units for an advanced science satellite. A year earlier, we held a Preliminary Design Review (PDR) of our proposed design. By all measures, it was a rousing success. We passed the review with flying colors, with the review team chairman congratulating me and my team for one of the best reviews he had chaired in some time. People stopped me in the hallways in the weeks afterward, congratulating me on what they had heard was an excellent job. Even my project manager, who was not known for being generous with his praise, told me I had done an excellent job and that I was one of his top development leads on the project. I was on top of the world.

Then it all came crashing down.

Being relatively new at NASA, I didn't have a lot of experience with the review process and the criteria for what was expected at each of the reviews. I didn't realize that the next review, the Critical Design Review (CDR), held roughly a year later, was a much more substantial review than the previous PDR that we had passed with flying colors. In fact, while the PDR was a much more top-level review, the CDR was a deep-dive and in-depth review intended to cover in detail the actual design as well as how we planned to build and test our units, and was the last "gate" before committing to build flight hardware. Needless to say, it was a significantly more detailed and stringent review than the PDR. Unfortunately, because of my inexperience, I didn't know this. Instead of the more detailed review required, I had my team instead provide a slightly more detailed version of the PDR we had presented a year earlier. As a result, we failed the review and failed it badly.

In truth, we didn't actually "fail" the review, at least not technically. Instead, the review chair (the same one who had praised me previously) stated that we had not met the criteria necessary to pass the review and assigned our team to go back and conduct a "delta" review. Essentially, this meant that we needed a "do-over" review to cover the deficient areas in the previous review, which was essentially the same as failing.

Word spread quickly among the project team about our failed review. Other subsystem teams quickly reviewed and shored up their own CDR presentations to avoid our humiliating fate. In my short career at Goddard, I knew of no other case where a team had to go back and repeat their review as we were directed to do. We became a cautionary tale to be avoided. As the team leader, the blame rested squarely on my shoulders.

I felt utterly humiliated. Here I was, a relatively new employee, trying to prove myself to a somewhat skeptical team (see **"You Have to Earn It"**) and, in this case, I did exactly the opposite. As a result, this failure devastated me. It was *the* most humiliating experience in my time at NASA. It felt, as I walked through my workplace, that people were whispering about me in the halls as I passed. I could only guess what my own team was saying behind my back. I wondered if I would ever recover from this major misstep.

Realizing that I had no choice but to move forward, I decided to "own" my failure. I went to people who I trusted and asked them to help me figure out where I had gone wrong. I made an appointment and sat down for a debrief with my review chair, who was tough but very helpful, and asked him to show me what we were missing from our failed review. I learned that NASA had specific criteria for each of their reviews and did my best to hunt down and understand this guidance. It was a difficult and humbling process, but I used this humiliating experience to regroup our team. Working closely with my team, we revised our presentation materials to reflect what was actually required for the review. When we held our "delta" review a month later, this time I had done my homework and we clearly passed, receiving authorization to move forward and start fabricating our flight units.

I never forgot that failed review and how I felt like a complete and utter loser. For a *long* time, it stung. But it did something else as well, something I didn't realize until later. I was never casual about reviews ever again. I became a student of reviews and why they were important. I took the time to understand what the purpose of each review was and what each was intended to illuminate. I became a virtual expert in the criteria for each review type and what these elements were intended to uncover. For every review since that failure, for the rest of my career, I developed a detailed review preparation package for each of my teams in advance of each review. This preparation package detailed the purpose of the review, a detailed roadmap of the preparations leading up to the review, and a checklist of topics and products that our team needed to develop and present for the review team. Eventually, as I became more experienced, I began sitting in as a member of review boards for other projects, working with the project teams to ensure that they understood their challenges and issues moving forward. Later, I started being sought out by other project teams as an outside advisor to help them prepare for their own reviews, working to "kick the tires" of their design and development approach before they actually entered the review itself. Over time, I had developed a real respect for the purpose and value of the review process and learned not to see reviews as a "check-the-box" requirement before moving on to the next stage of a project. Instead, I learned to see independent reviews as a valued tool for outside eyes to carefully examine and double-check the fundamentals of a mission design and the team's work, ensuring that they understood the challenges and were ready before moving on (see **"Someone Looking**

Over Your Shoulder"). None of this would have happened had I not failed that review almost 30 years ago. In retrospect, looking back, I am very glad that I failed that review (although I certainly didn't have that view back then). As hard as it was, it was a wake-up call that shook me up, took away my complacency, and made me a far better engineer and leader.

My experience has shown me that with every mistake there is always an opportunity for redemption, and out of the ashes of every failure is the opportunity for growth. Admittedly, it can be very tough at times, but there are rewards in the end for those who are willing to travel that tough path. Everyone makes mistakes, but not everyone successfully picks themselves up afterward. Abraham Lincoln has been quoted to have said, "I am not concerned that you have fallen—I am concerned that you arise." There is a Japanese proverb that says, "Fall down seven times, rise up eight." The *Book of Proverbs* similarly states, "A righteous man falls seven times, yet rises again." There is a common truth in all these quotes and sayings—we *all* fail at some point in our lives and careers, it's inevitable. The only way you are guaranteed never to fail is to never try anything, and the more challenges you accept that stretch you beyond your comfort zone, the more likely that, at some point, you will fail and maybe fail big. It's how we respond that makes the difference.

Knowing how to move forward after failure can be hard to figure out, especially when you are fresh off of a failure or a significant mistake. With this in mind, I have listed some suggested steps to consider after a major misstep or failure at work (which apply for failures outside of work as well).

- **Pick yourself up:** This is perhaps the hardest step to take, since this is the first one after your failure and, frankly, you may not feel like it. That's why it is so important. Find a way to pick yourself up and begin the recovery process. Depending on you, your personality, and how big (or small) your mistake was, this may either be a small step for you or a really, really big deal. The harder you've been knocked down (especially if it was your "fault"), the harder it is to get back up. Either way, it's important to find a way to pick yourself up and start moving forward again. One thing that can help you in the process is to talk to more senior people who you trust and respect and ask them about their biggest failures. If you do this (which I recommend), you'll quickly discover that these people you look up to probably had some pretty big whoppers of their own in their past, failures that knocked the wind out of them as well. Listening to their stories and how they recovered from their failures will make you feel better, let you know that you're not alone, and may even give you tips to add to your own recovery roadmap.

- **Take ownership and don't blameshift:** It's human nature to look to find blame, especially if it takes the focus off of ourselves. We all do it. Resist this urge with everything inside you, even if others may partially be at fault. Leave it to others to figure out where blame can be laid, that's not your job and shouldn't be your focus. Even in the case of my own failed review, it was clear that the blame was not all mine, especially with almost 30 years of looking back and revisiting it with more experienced eyes (yes, I still think about that failure!). As a young engineer just starting at NASA, there's no question that *someone* should have come alongside a green young engineer like me to make sure that I was preparing properly for that review, or at least review my materials prior to their presentation to make sure the contents "answered the mail". This is standard practice today and didn't happen then, and some could have argued that this omission set me up for failure. However, I didn't focus on that. Even back then, I knew that I needed to admit and "own" my failure, and it would have been unseemly for me to try to blame others for my mistake. A leader needs to take responsibility, not let things roll downhill (see **"Don't Let Things Roll Downhill"**) and it's never an effective strategy to point fingers. Instead, I took my lumps, swallowed hard, and decided that I would "own" this mistake and move forward.

- **Look for lessons learned:** There is something to be learned from every mistake. Make it your mission to find out the lessons to be learned in your particular situation. Begin the process to figure out what went wrong, why you think it went wrong, what could have been done differently to avoid this mistake, and what should be done in the future. Keep in mind that this could devolve into finger pointing and remember that this is *not* your goal. As a leader, you need to remain above any finger pointing and be solution oriented. As a practical matter, this is also how you will get the most honest and helpful answers from other people supporting you in this investigation. If people suspect you are looking for a scapegoat or someone to blame, they will circle their wagons and become defensive. However, if they are convinced you are not looking to lay blame but instead just want to get to the bottom of things, they are more likely to be honest and provide information, even if it may not cast them and their work in the best light.

- **Learn from your mistakes:** It has been said that "Those who cannot remember the past are condemned to repeat it." Mistakes that provide valuable lessons are building blocks to future successes. It is not enough to have "lessons-learned", these need to lead into the next steps of actually doing things differently down the road. I'm always impressed when members of review teams, all extremely experienced experts, warn our project team of potential pitfalls we may face down the road. One day, it dawned on me that they were *not* saying, "We did everything right and we want to make sure that you do so too!" I realized what they were *really* saying was "We really messed up in this area, and we want to warn you so that you won't make the same mistakes we did." People who make mistakes—and learn from them—go on to become great leaders, reviewers, and mentors. People who make mistakes and don't learn from them become cautionary tales that others are warned about. It may be that, for some mistakes or failures (like mine), there may be a need to develop a recovery plan or something similar to "make things right". Developing a collection of lessons learned will be instrumental to this activity. Even if there is no need

for a recovery plan, working through those lessons learned is an important step in learning where you went wrong and avoiding that pathway in the future.
- **Move on:** No matter how big your mistake, it is important to find a way to move on. It may take a while, but you'll be better off after learning from your mistake and continuing your journey forward. Everyone makes mistakes, and time will help put things into perspective.

If handled properly, almost any failure has the potential to eventually springboard you forward, becoming a strength area that you can refer back to down the road and allowing you to see how far you've come. Or it can remain simply a failure that you don't like to talk about or learn from. The choice is yours.

Guiding Principle: Everyone fails from time to time. The only people who don't fail are those who don't attempt anything difficult. The more difficult the challenge a person attempts, the more likely a failure may occur. The way we respond to failure is what differentiates those who simply fail from those who learn from their failures and actually turn them into strengths down the road.

CHAPTER 28

The Art of Negotiation

If you go into a technical field like engineering, I was told, you'll work primarily with technical challenges. You won't have to deal with much of the interpersonal interactions (and issues) that other career fields have to endure.

Then I started working. Now I can tell you for a fact that this is completely untrue. Any career that requires you to interface with other people (including your boss, and everyone has one) also requires you to deal with the complex interpersonal interactions that dealing with other people inevitably brings.

For example, I am often surprised, for a technical field, how much negotiation with people was involved in my NASA work. It was often challenging to build productive partnerships and agreements. One would think that we were all focused on the same thing—mission success—but the process of building those partnerships often seemed like a series of backroom negotiations. Some groups were willing and even excited partners, while some always seemed to want to engage in bargaining, hoping to see what they could get out of the deal for their group. Some wanted hiring points to bring in new hires, some had some favorite new technologies that they wanted to fly, some wanted to procure new equipment—the list seemed endless. In most cases, we were able to quickly get on the same page, but there were occasions where the negotiations were quite difficult.

On one mission, there was a negotiation with a technical group that was extremely challenging. These folks were annoying me so much that, if I was completely honest with myself, I finally reached the point where I didn't want to give them a win, even if it would cause me problems down the road. As a result, I seriously considered walking away from them so I wouldn't have to deal with them any longer. I visited a mentor of mine and loudly expressed my frustration, fully expecting that he would be firmly on my side and encourage me to walk away. Instead, he surprised me. While he sympathized with my frustration, he looked me in the eyes and told me that I was wrong. He gently reminded me that the mission required a highly diverse technical team, and every part of that team was needed to effectively design and complete the mission, even this group that was currently annoying me to death. He concluded by telling me that I needed to go back, re-engage with this group, and come up with something that I could say yes to. He expressed confidence that, once I put my emotions aside, I would be able to re-engage this challenging team and close the deal.

I was annoyed. I expected my mentor to be on my side—and was unhappy that he wasn't (as an aside, I have learned that the most valuable mentors are the ones who aren't afraid to tell you that you're wrong, even when it makes you mad). After I cooled down, I saw my mentor's point and went back to talk to this annoying group whose support, as my mentor frustratingly pointed out, I actually did need. We were able to eventually come to an agreement and they ultimately became an invaluable part of our mission and its success.

This was not the last tough negotiation I had to undertake as part of my role leading mission development teams. There were many other times when I was forced into extended discussions with technical teams in order to work out the details of their support for a given mission. These were mostly cordial discussions, though sometimes they were not. Whenever possible, I worked hard to be fair and to make these win-win situations for both sides, where everyone got something that they wanted. Sometimes, however, the negotiations were tougher and, as a result, I had to be tougher as well.

Negotiation can be painful. With some people, it is even more painful than normal. In the worst cases, it's not enough that they "win" and get what they want, it seems like they want to make sure that you lose as well. No one warned me that these sorts of interpersonal negotiations would be an integral part of my technical leadership role at NASA. I certainly didn't train for this and was forced to pick this up in real time, as part of my "on-the-job training".

The person who became my inspiration in learning the process of negotiation is my lovely wife. Over the years, as mother and a kindergarten teacher, she has become a master negotiator. If you have ever tried to negotiate with a young child, you know how frustrating that can be (one could argue that negotiating with some adults is akin to negotiating with a young child, but I digress). When my own children would argue with me about something they wanted to do, but something I didn't agree with, I had one negotiating tool—the word "No". I was a poor negotiator and it didn't always go very well.

But my wife, who was a *far* more experienced negotiator than I was and cut her teeth in the trenches of her kindergarten class, saw my shortcomings and taught me an invaluable principle—always find something that you can say "Yes" to. With this approach, rather than just saying "No", you instead offer in response one or more choices of things that you are willing to say "Yes" to. Saying "No" stops the negotiation process, but offering a "Yes" option demonstrates good faith, a willingness to come to a consensus, and keeps the negotiation moving forward in a constructive manner. I watched her do this with my children and it was amazing how much more effective this approach was than my more autocratic approach. It was not perfect, of course—the children still were unhappy when they didn't initially get their way, but it was surprising how much more quickly we arrived at a solution using this approach.

I adopted this "kindergartener-tested" approach at work and was surprised how helpful it was there as well. Rather than just saying "No" (which admittedly, I was prone to doing), I worked hard to instead offer one or more alternatives that I could say "Yes" to, either as an initial position or in response to a proposal I couldn't accept. I eventually realized two distinct advantages to this approach. First, it demonstrated a willingness to find compromise and opened the door to meaningful negotiation among two parties. Second, it changed my own mindset in negotiating with others. I realized that I was much more of a "No" person than I realized (although my kids could have probably told you that), which made me a poor negotiator. Using this approach helped change my thought process to one where I began every negotiation looking for avenues of compromise that could get us to "Yes".

It is worth mentioning that there are times when you may actually have to say "No" and stick to your guns. For some people, saying "No" is harder than saying yes and they just can't seem to do it. Learning to respectfully but firmly say "No" is one of the hardest things for some people to do. I recall a few years back when one of my sons was home by himself when a door-to-door charitable solicitor rang our front doorbell. Our son is one of the kindest souls possible and hates to say no. The charity representative at our door, likely sensing this, pounced on it and was able to get him to make a very sizable donation, one my son later regretted, feeling taken advantage of. When I asked him why he simply didn't say "No", he confessed that he simply didn't know how to politely do that and felt trapped. We had a long talk afterward on how, for some people, respectfully saying "No" in a polite and firm manner is one of the most challenging things to learn to do. It is an essential skill, though, to prevent people from unduly taking advantage of you. We talked earlier about the importance of finding something that you can say "Yes" to, but it is just as important to only say "Yes" when you feel like it and *not* because you don't know how to say "No" when you should.

Virtually every job—even technical ones—if they require you to interact with people, has some degree of negotiation embedded somewhere. Learning how to interact and negotiate properly is an invaluable skill, one that is established and reinforced through regular practice and on-the-job training. Growing in these skills will be a significant help in the workplace and allow you to properly assert yourself to ensure that you represent yourself and your positions well.

Guiding Principle: Even the most technical disciplines have some degree of negotiation inherent in their job description. Building skills to negotiate fairly and comfortably with others will enhance your job skills and allow you to properly assert yourself and represent your positions and goals. Always work to find something you can say "Yes" to, but also learn how to say "No" rather than succumb to undue pressure. Balancing these two skills will take time and practice, but will help you better navigate the negotiation process.

CHAPTER 29

Fear Versus Loyalty

I recall during a break in a leadership meeting one of the managers posed a question to our assembled group. "Which do you think is the greater motivation for an employee at work?" he asked, "Fear or loyalty? And by 'fear'," he added, "I mean leaving the employee constantly wondering where they stand with you, a sort of 'What have you done for me lately' environment where, as a result, the employee constantly works hard to stay in their boss' good graces."

"That's easy," I answered. "Loyalty is obviously the better motivator. It's also a far better way to treat the people working for you."

Most of the people (engineers) nodded in agreement. "Not so fast," said the manager, holding up his hand. He went on to vigorously argue that leaving employees always a bit on edge and wondering where they stand is actually the better motivator, as it causes the employees to constantly strive and push themselves to try to seek their management's approval. No amount of argument could persuade him otherwise.

I was stunned, having for the first time gotten this glimpse of this leader's management philosophy, and was shocked that we were even having this conversation in the 21st century. I just always assumed that everyone thought the way that I did, that building loyalty among a team was the best policy and the best motivator. This was the first instance where I realized that everyone did not share this perspective. Over the years, as I continued through the working world, I saw more and more instances where this "fear-based" philosophy had taken root. One senior manager I once worked for, in a moment of honesty, shared with me that this was his core management philosophy. He told me that, as a general practice, he withholds praise and encouragement so that his employees would always wonder where they stood. This manager was convinced that this approach would result in unsure workers continually striving for his affirmation and that this was the path to get the very best effort out of them.

I came to realize that this "fear-based" management approach was much more prevalent than I had originally assumed. I found it interesting that most of the proponents of this motivational philosophy tend to be managers, but most engineers I spoke to (who were the recipients of this policy) clearly felt that loyalty was a superior motivator (there's a lesson worth pursuing here, I think).

Let me forcefully state that I totally disagree with this "fear-based" motivational approach. I believe that this is clearly one of the lies of the workplace that needs to be dispelled. Instead, I firmly believe that loyalty is by far the superior motivator. I've had the opportunity to work under a variety of managers, some who clearly emphasized the "loyalty-based" approach and some who espoused the "fear-based" approach, and I've had the chance to observe the effects of both. The "fear-based" approach, where a manager withholds their affirmation in the hopes that an employee will always strive for approval, does have some short-term effectiveness. In the end, however, workers eventually see through this and become "9 to 5" workers, doing just enough to do their jobs and keep their noses clean. On the other hand, "loyalty-based" workers will become committed to their leader and their leader's goals, always willing to go the extra mile in support of leaders they feel loyalty toward.

These two approaches also have an impact on recruiting and retaining good people on the team. I once worked under a manager who subscribed to the "fear-based" philosophy described above. This approach did work—for a while. Eventually, the workers started to see through the façade, stopped trusting him, and lost their motivation. This manager later had trouble staffing his tasks once the workers got wise to his shenanigans. On the other hand, those managers and leaders who implemented an approach where they instilled loyalty through their honest and straightforward dealings with their workers were consistently able to get the best performance from their workers. These leaders' standards were high, and they expected the best from their employees, but they rewarded this with loyalty and received it back in return. These managers never seemed to have trouble staffing their projects. I believe, in general, you will get out of a relationship what you put in. If you don't treat your workers well, eventually that's what you will receive in return. Conversely, loyalty to workers results in a return of the same.

Another area to consider with these two approaches is how each will cause workers to respond when things on the project get tough. My personal experience indicates that the loyalty-based approach will still result in the best performance from workers, even in the midst of difficult circumstances. On one mission, I worked under a project manager who I grew to admire greatly. She was tough but fair and always treated the team with respect and made it clear how much she appreciated the hard work of the team. Over the course of the mission, the team developed a strong sense of loyalty toward her, myself included. On this mission, we had one component vendor that was very problematic in every possible way. To say that they were hard to work with would be an understatement. While the vendor's component was critical to our mission, the company was rude, they concealed information from us when it suited them, and I caught them being dishonest on more than one occasion. They were one of the most difficult vendors I had ever worked with. Finally, I had enough. After one particularly onerous interchange, I marched into the project manager's office and told her that we needed to fire them and get another vendor on board instead. She listened quietly, told me that it was too late in the schedule for that, and we needed to make things work with this vendor. She then went on to tell me that she wanted me to be the personal liaison to this vendor to smooth things over and ensure that they would deliver as planned. I shook my head violently and angrily refused. I told my project manager bluntly and in no uncertain terms that there was no amount of money in the world that she could pay me to take that assignment. She looked me dead in the eye, told me that she understood, and then asked me if I would do it instead as a personal favor to her. After a *long* moment of silence, I agreed. What I would never have done for money or a promotion, I was willing to do in response to a personal request by someone who had earned my loyalty. In fact, I willingly worked with that incredibly difficult vendor until they finally delivered their flight components solely because someone who I respected and felt personal loyalty toward asked me to do it as a personal favor. And *that* is the power that loyalty has in building a team, one that manipulative techniques will never be able to match. People will do things out of a sense of loyalty that they will never do otherwise.

There is an important point to make here, one that should go without saying—loyalty, like trust, is earned. You have to have a track record of consistent, demonstrated behavior in order to earn the loyalty of the people working for you. If you have not done this, don't be surprised if loyalty is in short supply in your organization. Too often, leaders demand loyalty from their workers without doing the upfront work to earn and establish it. Loyalty is a two-way street—to develop loyalty in those you work with, you have to first show it yourself. Loyalty is not automatically bestowed because people work for you— that sounds a lot more like "fear" than loyalty.

I am a strong believer in being honest, straightforward, and fair in my dealings with other people, and I hope and expect that other people will treat me in the same manner. I believe that manipulative tactics to try to motivate people are not only ill-advised, but they don't work in the long term. I believe that the "Golden Rule," which tells us to treat others the way we want to be treated, is still the best way to treat others, not only because it is right, but it also happens to be good business and a wise management approach. I have seen over the years that managers who adopt these approaches generally do well and have a loyal cadre of workers. I have also seen that managers and leaders who use clever and manipulative tactics to try to motivate their workers eventually develop a negative reputation, with workers recognizing their true colors and eventually resulting in people choosing not to work with them. With all other things being equal, most workers would prefer to work under those who value them by treating them with dignity and respect, while they would prefer not to work under those who disrespect them by playing mind games. Loyalty also continues to reap dividends after the project is over, as team members will continue to want to work with you and support you in the future (see **"Building Your Community"**).

I find it surprising that we even have to work through this discussion, as I feel that treating people in a way that instills mutual loyalty is always the standard that we should aspire toward. Alternatively, I believe that the "fear-based" alternate approach in the workplace promotes a destructive and ineffective workplace environment and is one of the workplace lies that needs to be exposed.

Guiding Principle: While there are ongoing debates on whether loyalty or "fear" is the better motivator, wise leaders come down squarely on the side of loyalty. Good leaders respect and inspire their workers, and loyalty is a natural by-product of this positive working relationship. The fruits of loyalty in a team are trust, hard work, and a willingness to go the extra mile beyond what is normally expected, making this an obvious positive attribute of any team culture.

CHAPTER 30

Don't Let Things Roll Downhill

Steve was one of my best electronic designers. He was meticulous, extremely conscientious, and painstaking in his work, and perhaps one of the best electronic designers at Goddard. Because he was so careful and conservative, Steve's flight electrical design work was always exceptional and performed well. He dotted every "*I*" and crossed every "*T*", and his work rarely had any errors. I felt extremely fortunate to have him on my flight avionics design team, working on a core segment of the spacecraft flight design.

It was this careful and meticulous nature that brought Steve to my office one day, and he was clearly stressed and worried.

We were in the midst of a "better, faster, cheaper" mission, where we were strongly encouraged to push new technology in ways we had never done before (see **"Drawing the Line"**). As a result, where we might normally use electrical components that had a long flight history and well-documented performance characteristics and data sheets, some of the components we were using on this mission had never been used before. Consequently, the components manufacturers were still figuring out the performance capabilities and design margins at the same time our designers were simultaneously implementing them into a flight electrical design. This was *not* the way Steve was used to operating and it was against his meticulous nature. Because of this approach, Steve was rightly concerned that incomplete component information could result in a design error that would need to be corrected later, resulting in cost and schedule impacts. Specifically, he was now standing in my office out of a very real concern that he would be blamed for any mistakes that resulted from the incomplete information that he was forced to use in his design efforts.

Steve and I talked this over for a long time and I could see that he was increasingly stressed by the difficult position he had been placed in—and was growing increasingly fearful of being blamed for any inadvertent mistakes that could result. Finally, I promised him, in no uncertain terms, that I would take full responsibility for any errors or mistakes that might occur—and that his name would never be mentioned in the event of any problems. I promised him that I would have his back. With this assurance, I encouraged him to instead focus exclusively on doing the best he could with the information he had available to him and not worry about the consequences. Steve looked very skeptical, but was willing to go back and complete his design with the assurances I had given him.

As Steve anticipated, despite his very best efforts, designing with incomplete information did result in an error, requiring cost and schedule impacts to fix. It didn't take long afterward, as the leader of our flight avionics team, that I was called into an angry manager's office to explain.

My manager, who was under intense pressure to avoid any schedule slippage, demanded to know who was responsible for the mistake. As I had promised, I took full responsibility. "It was me," I declared, explaining that the error was not the fault of a stupid mistake, but due to the inherent challenges of designing with still-emerging information on cutting-edge components. My manager, knowing that I was not an electronics designer but leading the team, continuously pressed me to reveal the actual offender so that he could "make an example of them," as if this would somehow make things right or dissuade future design errors. I remained steadfast and resolute, insisting it was my responsibility alone. We were at an impasse, the manager wanting to know who he could blame and I unwilling to expose my faithful worker to his wrath. Finally, after a long standoff, he backed off and we were able to focus on the real task at hand, which was to work on getting back on track. Steve, as he always did, quickly recovered, successfully completed the design, and contributed immensely to a successful mission.

I share this story for a reason. A project manager who I once worked for and respected greatly had a saying that he was fond of repeating—

"Never let things roll downhill." I found this to be a curious saying and it took me a while to figure out what he meant by this. I eventually deciphered its meaning. He was essentially saying that his job as a leader was to protect his team from troubles and distractions that were coming down from above, not letting these issues "roll downhill" to the workers on the team and defocusing them from their vital work. Instead, he saw his job was to serve as a much-needed buffer, leaving the team free to focus on the tasks before them. As a leader, he would regularly "take one for the team" so that the team wouldn't get distracted from their true priorities. It was a thankless but necessary job if the team was to keep moving ahead without continually getting distracted.

There is a common phrase in our culture, made popular by President Harry Truman, that states "The buck stops here." This phrase epitomizes a leader taking full ownership of a situation or problem and not passing the responsibility or the negative impact down the line to others. Sadly, this appears to be a rare quality these days, where many leaders are willing to "pass the buck", shifting blame and passing responsibility or consequences on to someone else in order to protect themselves. This is a type of workplace lie about leadership, one that does not represent true leadership, and needs to be called out for the negative example that it represents.

We live in a time when people misunderstand what it truly means to be a leader. Too often, people think that leadership is about being in control and ordering people around. In reality, true leadership is about articulating a vision, helping a team get invested and "buy into" this vision, and creating an environment and a pathway for the team to move steadily forward toward implementing that vision. An essential aspect of leadership is creating an environment that minimizes the obstacles that distract the team from implementing the vision. This is where "not letting things roll downhill" is so important. It is the leader's job to protect their team from unwanted drama and distractions that could blunt or defocus the teams' efforts, even if it means leaders have to take on the brunt of these distractions themselves. Leaders who let things "roll downhill" onto their teams are not fulfilling their leadership responsibilities and are doing their teams a grave disservice. Keeping things from "rolling downhill" doesn't mean simply ignoring outside inputs that could disrupt the team. Instead, it is the role of the leader to collect these inputs, often coming down from above, carefully assess and filter them, and provide clear direction to their team on anything that is relevant to them and their work. While this can be an unenviable and thankless job, it is a core aspect of true leadership.

The very nature of spacecraft and mission development at NASA often entails significantly pushing the state of the art. The challenges NASA missions face often require bold, out-of-the-box thinking in order to come up with new and unique solutions to solve problems that have never been tackled before. As a result, there is the ever-present possibility of wrong turns and errors, requiring the team to "go back to the drawing board" from time to time to figure out alternative ways to tackle difficult problems. It is certainly not a job for the timid or faint of heart, but rather requires a measure of boldness and risk. In order for teams to be bold, workers need to know that the leadership above them has their backs and will support them in the event that problems occur. This knowledge of support from above gives a team the confidence and the boldness necessary to do challenging, cutting-edge jobs. If a team has any doubts that the leadership is not 100 percent fully behind them, this knowledge will likely cause them to be overcautious and fearful, and may make the difference between successful innovation and failure.

Years later, I recalled my episode with Steve when I found myself in a similar situation. As the lead systems engineer on a large mission, I was leading the effort to test and verify our newly assembled spacecraft, and, as always, the schedule was breathing down our necks. We had two options for performing a specific set of tests—a slower, more traditional, and cautious approach, or a more innovative and aggressive "higher-risk, higher-return" approach that, if it worked, would save us substantial schedule time. However, if everything didn't go well with this higher-risk approach, it would mean backtracking to the traditional approach, with vital time lost and putting us further behind. A cautious approach would certainly dictate that we follow the slower, more traditional approach. My project manager approached me, though, and asked me to consider trying the bolder, higher risk, more innovative approach that could save us time. When I expressed concern about the optics of failing the test and falling further behind, she asked me to consider taking the risk, promising that she would have my back, no matter what happened. Because she had earned my loyalty (see **"Fear Versus Loyalty"**) and I trusted that she would indeed have my back, it gave me the confidence to be bold in implementing this alternate approach. Fortunately, it was fully successful and we were able to shave valuable time off the schedule. The assurance that I had in a trusted leader gave me the confidence to be bold and take measured risks that I probably would not have taken under someone I trusted less.

Good leaders establish trust with their team, protect their people, and "don't let things roll downhill", allowing their team to remain focused on the tough job at hand. While this often means that the leader is put in uncomfortable and unenviable positions themselves, it is an essential quality of good leadership.

Guiding Principle: Wise leaders "don't let things roll downhill". Instead, they protect their team from issues and distractions that can sidetrack and defocus busy workers from the critical job ahead of them. Good leaders run interference for the team and occasionally take the hit for the good of the team. When a team knows that their leader has their backs, it provides them with confidence to approach difficult challenges in a bold and innovative manner that they might otherwise approach with fearfulness and undue caution.

CHAPTER 31

No Stupid Questions Allowed

It was not long after I joined my latest project team that I realized there was something that was off, I just couldn't put my finger on it right away. After a period of careful observation, I finally figured it out.

The technical team was a great group of highly skilled engineers and managers, all excellent at what they did. But there was something obvious missing—there were no questions asked in the group meetings. In most of the teams I had been a part of, there was a regular "give-and-take" of people asking questions in every meeting in order to educate themselves on a particular issue or to better understand an area they were unfamiliar with. Not on this team. There was almost a complete absence of questions in open meetings, almost as if people were afraid of asking them. I soon found out why. The team had a few strong personalities who were very smart—they knew it and everyone else did as well. I noticed that whenever someone would ask a question that these individuals thought was beneath them, these strong personalities would subtly give signs that they thought the question was stupid, either through silent disapproval or a subtle comment that clearly communicated their disappointment in the question and the questioner. The other team members learned very quickly that asking a question came with the strong possibility of exposing themselves to subtle disapproval. As a result, the team environment quickly became a "no-question zone", which, without realizing it, became an unfortunate distinctive element of their team culture (see **"Creating a Team Culture"**).

I knew that any team that didn't ask questions was actually hindering open and free communication, which was very risky to the mission (see **"A Failure to Communicate"**). With this in mind, I immediately set out to dismantle this negative aspect of the team culture. I did this by asking questions—a lot of them. Every time I didn't understand something (and sometimes even if I did), I would ask a question. Oftentimes, these queries were met by obvious silent disapproval by the "question police", which I ignored, pretending to be oblivious. Slowly, others started asking questions as well, which I *always* complimented and used to initiate a more in-depth technical discussion, trying to model the principle that questions serve as an important "jumping-off point" for valuable technical discussions. It took a long time, but we were eventually able to steer that culture from a "no-question zone" to one where questions were tolerated and even encouraged.

Creating an environment where questions not only are tolerated but encouraged is a vital part of any healthy organization. The leadership of an organization needs to do all that it can to create this type of environment. Unfortunately, sometimes we can discourage questions without even realizing it. In some major project reviews that I attended, someone would invariably ask a question, starting somewhat hesitantly by saying, "This may be a stupid question, but…" Whenever someone would use this phrase, a respected senior technical expert I knew always made a point of immediately jumping in and stating, "There are no stupid questions, only stupid people who ask them." This line always got a good laugh among everyone in the room (I laughed too), but I always cringed a bit inside, worried that this humorous response actually served to dissuade others from openly asking other questions later in the review.

There's a train of thought in the workplace today that suggests that asking questions exposes you as someone who doesn't really know what they're talking about, and that "smart" people don't ask questions. This is a lie and nothing could be further from the truth. In fact, the opposite is true. Smart, well-informed people are confident enough that they are not afraid to ask questions and encourage questions in the workplace.

In my experience, a team that encourages questions among themselves is a healthy team. There is always someone who, for whatever reason, doesn't understand something as well as the others and a healthy team will graciously work to bring everyone up to speed. On the other hand, a team that discourages asking questions is an unhealthy team, hindering open communication, and running the risk of setting themselves up for problems down the road. Anything that creates a barrier to open communication and healthy questioning must be vigorously stamped out. When we create a culture that says "No stupid questions are allowed," what we are *really* saying is that *no* questions are allowed. All questions are "stupid" to someone, and limiting or eliminating them cuts off vital communication and learning among the team. After all, every team is staffed by a variety of people in different stages of their careers—the senior "graybeard" experts down to the entry-level engineers. A healthy team provides an environment where the senior people mentor the younger, less experienced ones. And this mentoring is done primarily by observing and asking questions, trying to understand "the reason why" things are done, and passing this knowledge down from the experienced leaders to the growing engineers. If cutting off questions occurs on a team, that team is starving a vital aspect of the learning and mentoring process. Sometimes that "stupid" question is the one that exposes a weakness in the approach that everyone else had missed. Creating a vibrant culture where everyone feels the freedom to question things is the surest way for issues and potential problems to be caught and addressed before they blow up into major challenges. Every team member can be enlisted to examine and question things that might have otherwise escaped unquestioned and unexamined, thereby creating a well-prepared team.

A well-prepared team has no need to fear questions, either from internal sources or from external reviewers. In fact, a good team will welcome all questions, either because the team has prepared well and has the answers or because the question will occasionally point out an area that the team may have missed. Responding to these "missed area" questions is a key purpose of external reviews and allows the team to correct the oversight and make their design or mission even stronger (see **"Someone Looking Over Your Shoulder"**). On one mission I helped lead, during a key design review, we had one reviewer who was asking an abnormally large number of questions. One of our senior technical leads, obviously annoyed, finally told this reviewer that he should stop asking so many questions and restrict his future questions to a narrower area of inquiry. Immediately, I could feel an icy chill go through the review team, their faces reflecting their displeasure with what they saw as interference in their independent review process. Restricting a review team from openly asking questions was certainly *not* part of the NASA review process and was a recipe for creating a disastrous adversarial relationship with any review team. As the lead systems engineer, I immediately stood and told the review team (and reminded our own team!) that any member of the review team could ask any questions that they wished on any topic, that we would be glad to either answer them on the spot or go off and research the answers if needed. Later, the review team chair came over and quietly thanked me, letting me know that my quick response had prevented the review from immediately going off the rails and turning adversarial. I was happy to make this stand, as I am a firm believer both in honest and penetrating questions and in the independent review process, and because I firmly believe that both make our missions better and more likely to succeed.

Creating a culture where questions are allowed and encouraged helps create an open environment where issues and potential technical problems are more likely to be uncovered sooner and chased to the ground. Additionally, it creates a sense of ownership among all the team members, where each individual sees themselves as responsible for bringing up any issues they see and being invested in their resolution.

Guiding Principle: Wise leaders work to intentionally create an environment that encourages everyone to ask questions and raise concerns to the entire team. This also creates a mentoring environment, where less experienced members learn from the more experienced ones, typically by observing and asking questions and passing down knowledge in the process. Any team that discourages asking questions creates an unhealthy environment that hinders open communication and risks hiding problems. Anything that creates a barrier to open communication and healthy questioning must be vigorously stamped out.

CHAPTER 32

Seeing the Big Picture

At the beginning of my second major NASA mission, I was still a "small picture" kind of guy. That is, I had a task right in front of me that I was responsible for accomplishing and that's as far as I could see. I was missing the "big picture" of the mission, but, like many "small picture" guys, I didn't realize it at the time.

Steve, on the other hand, was the opposite. Like me, he was one of the key technical leaders on the mission, and his role, like mine, was essential to our mission success. Unlike me, however, he could clearly see the big picture, even in the beginning at the formative stages of the mission. He knew our next mission was going to be a big one and he would tell us this all the time. "This mission is going to revolutionize our understanding of the universe," he would tell me over and over again for the next few years. "We are lucky to be involved in such a game changing mission!" I would politely smile and nod, but I was much more worried about getting our design team moving, trying to overcome our current technical challenges, and meeting a tough schedule.

It was only much later in the mission development effort that I slowly understood the importance of our mission and, if we were successful, how it would expand our understanding of cosmology (the science of the origin, evolution, and structure of the universe). That mission, the Wilkinson Microwave Anisotropy Probe (WMAP), went on to successfully complete highly precise measurements of the cosmic microwave background (i.e., residual electromagnetic radiation from the Big Bang, the time when the universe began). Papers citing the WMAP results became the most referenced science papers in physics and astronomy. *Science* magazine declared that the WMAP mission was the *Breakthrough of the Year for 2003,* and the WMAP Science Team was later awarded the 2018 Breakthrough Prize in Fundamental

Physics.[*] Physicist Stephen Hawking called WMAP science results supporting the cosmological theory of inflation "the most exciting development in physics during his career."[†] My co-worker Steve was right—the WMAP mission results really were a big deal in the world of science, and the mission truly was a game changer.

Between Steve and me, one of us clearly saw the "big picture" game-changing possibilities from the very beginning of the mission—and how the science results from our mission would revolutionize our understanding of the universe. And it wasn't me, at least not at first. I was more concerned about keeping my head down, meeting my mission obligations, and not being the "weak link" of the project.

That mission was a huge wake-up call for me. It taught me the importance of opening up my eyes and trying to understand the "big picture" purpose of what I was doing, rather than staying a "small picture" kind of guy. "Big picture" thinking is being able to see the importance of the end results and how your work contributes to that end. Seeing the big picture not only motivates and inspires you, it also gives you a practical understanding on how your "piece" fits into the larger scheme of things, why it is important, and how to improve your work to enhance the chances of "mission success".

Some people believe that seeing the "big picture" is really not all that important. After all, you have a job to do, just do it! These people believe that, for a good and faithful worker, no extra motivation is required, and it can distract from the job at hand. I believe that this is a common workplace falsehood and couldn't be further from the truth. As we'll see, understanding the big picture not only can be a source of additional motivation, but also can provide valuable context to help guide an individual's work in order to be more focused and effective.

My experience reminds me of a well-known story that is based on an actual true-life event. After a great fire ravaged much of London in 1666, the world-famous architect Christopher Wren was commissioned

---

[*] https://map.gsfc.nasa.gov/.
[†] Grossman, L. December 18, 2012. "2013 Smart Guide: New Maps to Rein in Cosmic Inflation," New Scientist.com, www.newscientist.com/article/mg21628965-700-2013-smart-guide-new-maps-to-rein-in-cosmic-inflation/.

to lead the rebuilding of St. Paul's Cathedral, which was destroyed in the fire. As the story goes, one day Wren was on the job and supervising the rebuilding effort and he came upon three bricklayers working on the rebuilding project. He asked them what they were doing and each of the three gave very different responses. The first bricklayer said, "I'm laying bricks." The second said, "I'm building a wall." The third said, "I'm building a cathedral." All three were bricklayers and all had the same job. The difference between these three men was the perspectives they had on their work. The first two bricklayers were "small picture" guys, while the third was a "big picture" guy who saw how his efforts fed into a grand purpose far above his day-to-day tasks. He had a clear vision of the end product that he was helping to work toward.

You may rightly ask, "What does it matter? Why should I care whether or not I or anyone else has a 'big picture' mentality?" Seeing the big picture helps move individuals from having a myopic view of their work and its value and refocuses their perspective to see how their work fits into larger goals and plans. A parenting book that I read years ago explained that it is always important to tell your children "the reason why" you're asking them to do something instead of just telling them to do it. Understanding "the reason why" has the potential to turn children from mindless rule followers into people who understand the context behind the rules they have been given and why following them is important. Understanding "the reason why" isn't just following orders. It creates learning opportunities and—in the process—expands a person's view of the world and why they do (and don't do) things. In the same way, when workers understand the "big picture" on a project or task, they are being given a greater understanding of "the reason why", widening their perspective of the purpose of their work and why it is important. This increased understanding may even enable them to contribute more toward the success of the task at hand.

Someone who understands the "big picture" of their work and the larger goals this work is a part of has a greater context as to the value of their work. This context separates them from those who simply report to work each day and do their job, and instead expands their perspective on their work and its purpose. This new expanded mindset turns them into thinkers with a greater ability to make contributions. Many times, on my spacecraft development teams, an engineer who understands the "big picture" has made suggestions or found problems that others have missed and is only able to do so because of an understanding of the larger mission and its goals.

In addition, having a "big picture mentality" can provide a greater vision for an individual on the importance of their work, potentially increasing their job satisfaction. I believe that all of us are looking for purpose and significance in our lives and, since we spend a huge portion of our lives at work, it would be nice to find it there as well. Looking at the case of the three bricklayers, I suspect that the third bricklayer went home each evening more inspired than the other two, as he had a larger appreciation of his work's purpose and the fruits of his efforts. In the same way, my co-worker Steve was much more excited each day than I was, knowing the potential our mission had to revolutionize mankind's scientific understanding of our universe. I believe most people want their work to matter and have significance rather than just pulling in a paycheck. Understanding how your work fits into the "big picture" can have a tremendously motivating effect and can significantly increase your job satisfaction.

A year before WMAP launched, our team held our L-1 (launch day minus one year) party. At this event, the mission's lead scientist stood up and gave one of the most inspirational talks I have ever heard at work. He talked about how he had been envisioning this mission concept for over 15 years and how hard it was to jump through the hoops to get it finally approved as a NASA project. He described the mission as his life's work. He went on to explain how, if successful, this mission would reverberate through the field of cosmology and explained the tremendous impact it would have. He thanked the assembled entire team, from the project manager down to the technicians, for being part of his vision and making it happen. It was an amazing talk—and it utterly ruined our L-1 party, because everyone was so inspired that they wanted to go back to work right then and make the mission happen! He had successfully imparted the "big picture" to the entire team and it was a tremendous motivator to everyone!

Sharing the "big picture", if done properly, can have a powerful effect on a team in reaching its goals, motivating them far beyond simply "doing a job". Not only can it expand the vision and understanding of the workers on the team, but it also can help them to grow and progress into greater responsibility and perhaps greater career opportunities.

Guiding Principle: Wise leaders always take the time to share the "big picture" to their teams—not just once, but over and over again. These leaders know that understanding the big picture not only allows their workers to become personally invested in the task at hand and gives valuable context to their work, but also makes them better contributors to the effort.

CHAPTER 33

Setting Boundaries

It was early in my career at NASA and I was working long hours just to try and stay on top of a steep learning curve and heavy workload. I wasn't unhappy, however. Working at NASA was my dream job and I wanted to do whatever it took to carry my weight and measure up to the high standards that I saw around me. I wanted to show people that I belonged here and I was willing to do whatever it took to demonstrate that. Doing this, however, often resulted in long workdays and typically working through lunch.

One day, Paul stopped me in the hallway. We worked on the same project and, although we were not on the same technical team, our labs were on the same hallway and we had become casual friends. He was a bit older (and wiser) than me and I appreciated picking his brain from time to time. This time, however, it was obvious that he had something on his mind.

He had been watching me and the frenzied pace I was keeping at work and was concerned. The workload here will eat you alive if you let it, he warned. He told me that, on his previous missions, there were always one or two divorces among the team members on the mission team. He wasn't suggesting that work was the sole cause of these breakups, but the pace and the workload undoubtedly added additional stress on home life and probably didn't help. He told me that he could tell that I was a family man and just wanted me to take care and be careful.

It was a bit of an odd exchange, very direct and seemingly out of nowhere, but I appreciated the warning and thanked him. In my head, however, I shrugged it off, knowing that it wouldn't be an issue for me and my growing family.

Fast forwarding a year or so, we were in the grip of a tight schedule and my team was (as always) behind schedule in delivering our flight avionics units to the spacecraft. There was an immense amount of pressure to bring in the schedule in order to keep the launch date. I told the leader of our program office, who I had always liked and respected, that I and my team would do whatever it took to deliver these units on time. In fact, I committed to him that we would literally work every day until both units were delivered.

And that's just what we did. Our team worked virtually every day for approximately three months until we delivered. And these weren't just 8-hour days, these were easily 12 to even 16-hour days, every day. I would leave early in the morning, before the sun rose, and get back late at night. As a result of these long work hours, there were times where I wouldn't see my young children while they were awake for a week at a time.

My wake-up call came one day when I woke up well before dawn (again) and tried to sneak out without waking up the rest of the family. As I was getting ready to head out the front door, my oldest son, who was five years old at the time, appeared at the top of the stairway, rubbing his eyes and half asleep. "Daddy, where are you going?" he asked groggily. I told him that I had to go to work and that he should go back to bed. Instead, he plopped down at the top of the steps and started crying. "Daddy, I *never* see you anymore," he said between sobs.

My heart just about broke. I picked him up and comforted him, but I knew I had to be quick because the team needed me at work and I didn't have much time. I thought about this all the way to work that morning, feeling absolutely terrible.

We eventually delivered the flight avionics units, the mission launched on time and it was very successful. But I had learned a lot in the process and finally understood what Paul was trying to warn me about months earlier. After launching, I sat down with my wife and apologized for what I had put our family through. I told her that there would always be brief crunch times when my work schedule would be crazy. That was the nature of my job. But I promised her that, if it looked like these crunch times would extend from weeks into months, I would quit and find another job. While there were quite a few busy times after that, nothing ever approached the extreme schedule we had just gone through. I made sure of that.

Our family was fine after that crazy extended work experience. My lovely wife and I didn't get a divorce, we remain happily married, and our entire family is tight-knit to this day. My adult children seem to be proud of my NASA career, despite my occasionally crazy hours. My oldest son, who was five years old back then, seems to be (relatively) undamaged from his childhood experience and we are very close. In fact, as I write this, he is getting ready to launch his second spacecraft as a flight controller on his own NASA mission. But I have noticed that he guards his work–life balance very carefully, making sure that time with his wife and children is a top priority. I can't help but wonder if this is a conscious or unconscious reaction to all the crazy hours I worked early in my career.

When I talk to younger engineers, I see the gleam in their eyes and their desire to prove themselves in the crucible of hard work, to conquer the world and to make names for themselves. I remember that look myself and I certainly felt the same way. And, like Paul did for me, I always remind them to be careful. I warn them that work will *always* gladly take as much as you are willing to give and that it is up to *you* to set the boundaries. If you don't set these boundaries yourself, no one else will.

In today's success-driven culture, working long hours and flirting with burnout seem to be the norm in the workplace. We're often told that, if we want to be successful, this will be our "normal"—the price that needs to be paid to achieve it. After allowing myself to be sucked into this type of frenetic workplace environment myself, I see it clearly now for what it is—that this is another lie in today's workplace and a false choice that employees are pushed to make under the guise of pursuing success. I read a quote the other day that really reinforced the choice—and the consequences—that each of us has to consider—"*20 years from now, the only people who will remember that you worked late are your kids.*" As someone who has worked numerous long hours over the course of my career, this was a sobering reminder to me that work, as important as it is, needs to be balanced with other things in life that are even more important.

To be frank, no job is worth compromising your family relationships, your mental or physical health, or just living a balanced, happy life. Ideally, our jobs should be vocations that bring us a sense of accomplishment and satisfaction, not places that undermine the stability of our lives. I don't believe anyone goes into a job expecting to trade their well-being against the demands of the job, but sometimes our jobs keep asking for more and, before we know it, we are out of balance. If you find yourself in that kind of situation, some self-assessment and perhaps a readjustment might be needed.

There are many things in our lives that are vying for our attention. The reality is that we can't do it all, as much as we may wish we could. Trying to do everything is a recipe for disaster. We need to find a way to prioritize things in order to keep our activities manageable and prevent overload. The way to do this is for each of us to consciously decide what is important, make these things our priorities, and live with the boundaries that we set to make this happen.

Over the course of our careers, there will be times when we push beyond our normal limits to meet a deadline, accomplish a goal, or otherwise test our limits. A manager I once worked for told me that these key moments in time are when we prove ourselves both to others and to ourselves, showing what we are made of, and I agree with him. We often look back on these types of events as "our finest hour" and we forge lasting bonds with our team members in the trenches during these times. But if they last too long, they can be detrimental and destabilizing.

Guiding Principle: Your work will *always* take as much as you are willing to give. It is up to you to set appropriate boundaries. If you don't set those boundaries, no one else will. Good leaders set appropriate work–life boundaries for themselves and for their teams, making sure that there is a proper balance needed for mental health and healthy personal lives, and to prevent personal issues and burnout.

CHAPTER 34

Burning Out

I loved my job at NASA (well, most days, at least). Working there was literally a dream come true. I got to see and work on things that I only dreamed of doing when I was a kid. My patient wife learned early in our marriage that, when conversations with our friends turned to my work at NASA, I could unknowingly dominate the conversation throughout the evening, talking enthusiastically about the amazing things we were working on and telling story after story about the various missions I had been exposed to. I was a true believer—NASA should have hired me as their public relations consultant.

Which is why, after many years on the job, my wife became concerned when I became listless and discouraged, seemingly having no energy for work—and with any work-related conversation sounding more and more like complaining.

I had been working long hours and was under a lot of stress. This was nothing new, as this seemed to be a perpetual part of my career, even though I had worked hard to cut back from my previous busy schedule (see **"Setting Boundaries"**). For some reason, this time was different. Where I could normally rise above the daily stresses and issues at work, this time it just seemed to drag me down. My normally positive demeanor changed into something darker and more discouraging. I couldn't put my finger on just what was wrong. I finally figured out what it was. I was suffering from burnout.

I had seen this at work before, especially in people who I knew who had high-profile and high-stress jobs, like many of my fellow mission systems engineers. I had seen normally positive and energetic people become discouraged and taciturn, oftentimes resulting in uncharacteristic outbursts at work. Many of these people would eventually move out of these high-pressure jobs, allowing themselves time to cool down and de-stress. Sometimes, they were in the middle of a job that didn't allow these kinds of breaks and they had to just keep marching forward. In some instances, unsympathetic upper management would simply throw these people, who were typically high performers, back into the pressure cooker of another job, seeing them as valuable assets who couldn't afford to be allowed to sit on the bench when work needed to be done.

Over the course of their career, anyone who has an even remotely challenging job will struggle with burnout. Burnout has been described as chronic work-related stress that has not been successfully managed and can affect a person physically, emotionally, and behaviorally. There are many signs of burnout, but a few of the key ones are exhaustion or a lack of energy; a poor attitude or apathy about your job, coupled with an increasingly negative or a cynical view of your work or workplace; significantly reduced effectiveness at work; and physical effects, such as anxiety, headaches, lack of sleep, or fatigue. These are all classic signs of burnout and, while I didn't have all of them, there was no question that I was exhibiting many of these characteristics.

In my case, I had been working long hours over a prolonged period of time. My role as a lead Mission Systems Engineer on my current project was stressful—much of the stress being a byproduct of the job, along with my own high goals and perfectionist tendencies. I was also working on a very high-profile mission with lots of visibility. However, I had been in these types of situations before and, while it was stressful and challenging, it had never led to burnout. I think that the difference this time around was an additional factor, that there were philosophical differences between the technical and management teams that were not getting resolved and were adding to an already challenging situation. Whereas in the past my managers were a support to me, in this case, my relationship with the management team was constantly a challenge and didn't offer any support and encouragement to help keep me properly grounded. Needless to say, I was under a lot of pressure. My normally positive disposition began to change.

As with most people suffering from burnout, it was the people closest to me who saw it first and noticed the changes. One of my managers, Karen, who I had worked with previously on NASA missions and was a longtime friend, was the first one to bring it to my attention.

I was sharing with her the challenges I was facing with the project and she stopped me and asked me how I was doing. We had known each other for years and had "grown up" working on many of the same flight missions together. She knew me well and knew something was not right.

But it was the person closest to me that made me face the fact that something was not right. One evening after work, my wife sat me down and we had a talk at the kitchen table, where she laid out her observations on my mood change and concerns about my work and my attitude. She revealed that my children were walking on eggshells around me, noticing my shortened fuse and lack of patience. She then said something to me that she had never said in all of our many years of marriage, even during times when I was working the craziest of hours. She asked me, for the first time, to find another job. She could see that this job was bad for me, I was suffering from burnout, and I needed a break. I was shocked at the request, and we talked long into the night. By the time we went to bed, I agreed with her assessment and knew I needed to make a change. I appreciated her intervention and her care for me in bringing it up. I began to plot my escape.

Because it was a big, high-profile project, the departure was not easy, and numerous people above me had to approve. But I had reached the point where I knew a change was absolutely necessary. Fortunately, I had followed my own advice and trained my replacements (see **"Training Your Replacement"**), and ultimately, after some high-level meetings, I was allowed to move on. I moved into another program office where I provided technical oversight over a number of fascinating missions, working alongside a management team I knew and admired greatly. It was a great transition and it wasn't long before I was my old self. Interestingly, when I ran into many of my co-workers, every single one of them commented to me about the change in my demeanor since my transfer. When I probed further, virtually all of them told me that they had noticed a negative change in how I was behaving when I was still in my old position and had been concerned that something was wrong, and now were delighted that the "old John" was back. Again, the person suffering from burnout is often the last to realize what is going on, and

I'm thankful that my faithful wife took the initiative to sit me down and have a tough talk with me.

Most of us don't want to share anything that looks remotely like weakness or doesn't present a glowing view of ourselves and I'm certainly no different. Talking about what I went through is not easy for me. However, seeing some of the people who I worked alongside and the stress that they were under, I think this is an important topic to cover. Burnout looks and smells like weakness to many. However, we need to recognize this for the workplace lie that it is. Having worked closely alongside many driven high performers, I've seen a lot of burnout during my career, and not one of the people who suffered from it could remotely be called weak. Sometimes, like me, people notice the signs and make a change. In some cases, I've seen that burnout continues unabated and becomes a full-fledged breakdown, and people I respect and admire simply crash, having pushed themselves too far. It's typically the highest performing people who are afflicted with this, pushing themselves harder than anyone else could possibly push them, and sometimes beyond their limits. The recovery for these people is long and hard, and sometimes they never quite recover to their previous state or abilities. I don't know whether or not my case would have progressed to this level if I had not made a change, but I'm glad I didn't have to find out.

After my transfer, I had the opportunity to work on some amazing missions and alongside some wonderful people. My normal enthusiasm was restored and I once again bored my long-suffering friends with endless NASA stories. Obviously, this move was absolutely the right one for me. It would have been nice if the larger engineering organization had been on the lookout for possible burnout signs in me and my fellow at-risk co-workers, but I have seen that most organizations tend to be understaffed and have a hard time letting their skilled workers take a break. Oftentimes, these organizations are simply insufficiently educated on the signs of burnout, making it difficult for them to see the symptoms and take action. It is a reminder that work will always gladly take as much as you're willing to give and that if you don't set boundaries, no one else will (see **"Setting Boundaries"**).

Guiding Principle: Burnout is a very real danger at work, especially among the hardest-working and most invested members of a team. The negative effects of burnout can seriously hurt these individuals and can injure and sideline these previously highly productive people. Wise leaders will be on the lookout for telltale signs and help their workers take a break as needed in order to prevent stressful conditions and long work hours from taking their toll.

CHAPTER 35

Sometimes the Problem Is Just Hard

Our team had been struggling for some time. It seemed like, for each step forward we were taking, we took two steps back.

Most NASA and commercial aerospace vendors who are involved in the spaceflight business will tell you that acquiring the flight electrical parts needed for the spacecraft avionics in a timely fashion is always an issue. Electrical parts intended for on-orbit use are required to undergo rigorous manufacturing and qualifications testing requirements, which lengthen their time to delivery. For our mission, these requirements were even tougher. It was a big mission, which made selecting and acquiring all of the parts within the needed time frames of our tight schedule even more difficult. Most electrical parts had obscenely long lead times, which is the time it takes to actually receive the parts once they are ordered. By the time the electrical designers had finished their final designs and told our parts engineers which electrical parts needed to be ordered, we were already pushing the schedule into dangerous territory. All it would take was a few parts deliveries to slip and the project could be in serious trouble.

Knowing this and the critical importance of the parts effort across our mission, as the lead systems engineer for the project I decided to take a personal role in this parts effort. I brought in the best parts engineer at Goddard, who I had worked with previously and who had impressed me immensely with his ability to work magic on parts procurements. But even this parts engineer was not enough to order and keep track of all the parts needed for this large mission. So I brought in another of Goddard's best parts engineers. Even with this addition, we were still swamped and falling behind. Finally, I brought in a third parts engineer, now having staffed my project with arguably the three best parts engineers at Goddard. I had a great professional and personal relationship with each of them and was able to cajole them into helping me out (see **"The Value of Relationships"**). I kept nervously waiting for other projects at Goddard to complain about me having cornered the market on the three best parts engineers on the Center and placing them on our project. I knew, however, that we were not going to solve our parts issues without the very best people and a lot of work (see **"The Right Man (or Woman) for the Job"**).

I started meeting multiple times a week with this experienced parts team, which had almost 100 years of combined parts experience between them. Still, we struggled—trying to order the parts, scheduling needed testing, and keeping track of supplier issues. Slowly, members of the project team started to grumble once they realized the impact that late parts deliveries might have on their schedules. The grumbling started spilling out into the larger project meetings, with technical leads and their designers starting to more openly blame me and my parts teams for possible delays down the road. Whenever these complaints would come up, I would clearly explain everything we were doing so that everyone would clearly understand that we were pulling out all the stops to meet parts need dates. However, that was little comfort when, despite our efforts, we couldn't show the progress that these technical teams wanted to hear. I honestly didn't know how to respond to these legitimate complaints. We were working as hard as we could but were still coming up short.

It was in one of these meetings that one particularly vocal electrical designer spoke up before the team, indirectly slamming me and the parts team for delays that were affecting their schedule. One of the managers leading the project listened to his recitation of complaints, which were becoming more commonplace. Finally, he spoke. "When I look at this problem," he began, "I agree, we're not where we need to be. However," he continued, "it seems to me that we have some of our project's best and brightest people working on this problem and we're *still* struggling with it. What does that tell me?" He paused for effect, looking around the room. "It tells me that it must be a pretty hard problem to solve."

I appreciated the vote of confidence immensely. His words eliminated the grumbling that was growing among members of the team, both in that meeting and afterward. But more than that, I appreciated the sense of perspective that he brought to the challenge we were facing. It *was* a tough problem, and we were doing everything we could to address it. This manager swiftly and effectively exposed and put to rest the common lie that suggests that if an individual or team is struggling with a problem at work, it must mean that someone simply isn't doing their job effectively. Sometimes, the problem is just hard and eludes an easy, convenient solution.

This should have been obvious to me, but it was much more of a revelation than I expected. I was used to powering my way through any problem that I faced at work, using a combination of out-of-the-box thinking, long work hours, and the best workers I could find. And I was mostly successful doing things in this manner. My manager's comments reminded me, however, that just because the results didn't turn out as smoothly as I or others wanted doesn't mean that the team was not working their butts off to solve it. Sometimes the problem is just hard.

I'm a bit embarrassed to admit that this experience changed my perspective fairly significantly. Previously, when I would see a team (not my own, of course) struggling with a problem, I admit that my first thoughts were not the most charitable. I would naturally assume that the team wasn't very skilled, wasn't working as hard as they could, or wasn't staffed properly for the challenge at hand. In some cases, these assumptions may have been true. But my recent and humbling experience taught me that sometimes the problem is just hard. When the problem is hard, even a great, hardworking, and well-staffed team can still struggle. Even as I write this down, it seems so obvious that I'm a bit embarrassed that I am repeating something that should be so clearly evident. But this newfound perspective was very enlightening. It is very easy to become a Monday morning quarterback and second guess why a team is struggling with persistent problems. Being in this position gave me a newfound perspective.

Our parts engineers continued to work miracles with the parts vendors, pulling in schedules and working with them to quickly resolve issues as they arose, which is why they were the best parts engineers on the Center. After many hours of work, we eventually got our arms around the parts deliveries and were able to meet our schedule. All flight units were delivered on time, we launched on schedule, and that science mission is still collecting valuable data to this day.

I learned a valuable lesson on that project that I carry with me to this day. When I see people struggling with a difficult problem at work or on another mission, I resist the urge to find fault and instead first try to understand the nature of the problem and its difficulty. Sometimes the team does have some shortcomings and needs help. But sometimes the problem is just hard.

Guiding Principle: When a team is struggling on a task, it is tempting to assume that the team isn't very skilled, is not working very hard, or is not staffed properly. However, sometimes the problem is just hard. When a problem is hard, even a great, hardworking, and well-staffed team can still struggle.

CHAPTER 36

Voting With Your Feet

Paula knocked on my office door and asked if she could speak to me. I could tell immediately from her tone and demeanor that something was up—and that it was *not* good. Unfortunately, I was right. Paula was coming to let me know that she was leaving our team. In fact, she was leaving Goddard as well, taking a job elsewhere.

This was a big loss for our project team, as well as a disappointment for me personally. Paula was a skilled engineer and a significant asset to my spacecraft development team. Hardworking and industrious, she was also quiet and soft-spoken, the kind of person who you always knew was thinking about things, her head churning with thoughts and ideas. Unlike others who would readily speak up in meetings, with Paula you could see the wheels turning and I often had to ask her what was on her mind before she would speak up. I appreciated her immensely and could see that she was going to grow into a significant player on our project effort. Now, unfortunately, she was leaving.

Her departure was a disappointment to me personally for another reason. I had always prided myself on my ability to keep my fingers on the pulse of the team, knowing how everyone was doing and working to diffuse issues behind the scenes before they flared up and caused problems within the group. Paula's announcement caught me totally by surprise. I had sensed that there were issues, but didn't think they were significant enough to warrant her departure. Her visit to my office told me in no uncertain terms that I had been wrong.

As always, Paula was polite and to the point. She felt that it was time to move on and she had found a great opportunity outside of Goddard and had decided to take it. She would be leaving in just under a month, enough time to wrap up her work and transfer her responsibilities to someone else on the team. Always gracious, she thanked me for the opportunities on the project and wished me well. I told her that I was very sorry to hear that she was leaving and asked if there was *anything* I could do to get her to stay. No, her mind was made up, but she appreciated me asking. I told her that she would be greatly missed.

Then I probed a bit further. While I understood that she had a great job opportunity elsewhere and that it would be good for her career, I wondered if there was anything on our team that she was unhappy with, something that was causing her to leave. No, she insisted, it was just a great opportunity and it was time to move on. I pressed further—typically, people don't look for outside opportunities and decide to leave unless there is something that they are unhappy with. I assured her that I wasn't trying to twist her arm to get her to stay. Rather, she would be doing me a favor if she could shed some light on possible issues on the team, perhaps something that I was missing that might cause a valued worker like her to decide to leave. I promised her that I would keep anything she shared private and only use it to try to correct any issues that I might have been missing.

Slowly, reluctantly, Paula admitted that there was something. There were some personality dynamics on the team that she was unhappy with, one person in particular who was difficult to work with. She had tried for some time to make it work but, despite her best efforts, it was clear that things were not improving. Finally, being the nonconfrontational type, she decided that it was easier to leave than to continue forward with the way that things were going.

I thanked her for her honesty and openness, promising to keep our conversation between us. In turn, she thanked me as well, indicating that I was the only one in her entire organization who had probed further and was determined to uncover if there were deeper issues that were causing her to leave. I'll never forget what she told me—"I guess it's just too painful or inconvenient for people to know the real, deeper issues why people are unhappy or choosing to leave, because then they'll have to *do* something about it. And most people would rather be left in the dark than actually have to try to address any underlying issues."

This exchange highlights a real and pervasive problem in most workplaces, where there are underlying issues in a team or organization that the leadership doesn't see or, if they do, doesn't want to address.

VOTING WITH YOUR FEET 193

Let's face it, dealing with issues is not fun—no one *wants* to have to dredge up underlying issues and work to correct them. As a result, most organizations ignore them or sweep them under the rug, unknowingly leaving them to fester and grow. Most workers in these types of organizations shrug, roll their eyes, and keep working, the issues remaining an open secret among most of the people in the group. Some employees, like Paula, reach their threshold, get tired of it, and "vote with their feet", meaning that they decide it's not worth it anymore and they leave. Like Paula, they may be publicly very positive and cordial about the reasons for their departure, and talk about "other opportunities" or "needing to spend more time with their families". However, by "voting with their feet", the words they are telling you are actually a polite veneer and they are actually unhappy enough that a big change is needed. Most of these people will not tell the leadership why they are really leaving because they think that it won't make any difference and it will just stir up too much trouble that they would rather avoid.

Leaders in the workplace mistakenly assume that if a worker is not happy, they will let you know before they decide to take the dramatic step of deciding to move on. This is simply not true. While this may occur in some cases, most workers are uncomfortable with the idea of approaching their supervisors and "making waves". In many cases, there is an organizational barrier between workers and their supervisors that may hinder such open communication (see **"Climbing Out of the Ivory Tower"**). Believe it or not, for many workers, it is easier to move on and leave the organization than it is to approach a supervisor with their concerns. It is up to the leader to regularly "take the temperature" of their team to keep track of how they are doing, hopefully with the goal of heading off any potential issues before they spin out of control.

People "vote with their feet" all the time. When they make a move, they are quietly telling you something that they are unwilling to say with their words. It takes a perceptive and determined leader to get them to open up about what they are really thinking, like I did with Paula. I've done the same thing myself. Once, when leaving a job, my supervisor asked me why I was leaving, and, instead of being honest, I gave the excuse that I was stressed and wanted to spend more time with my family, rather than talk about the miserable working environment of my job. The reasons I did this were (1) I wanted out and I knew this was the easiest way to get there and (2) I knew that this supervisor really didn't want to know if there were problems on the job and wasn't going to do anything meaningful to correct them. It was easier to "vote with my feet". If my supervisors knew me at all, they would have known that there was more afoot and would have dug deeper like I did with Paula, but they didn't. Had my supervisor or others taken the time and interest to honestly dig deeper and show that they were interested in making changes, there was a great deal I could have told them about underlying issues in that organization that needed changing, but instead it went left unsaid.

In Paula's case, I felt I missed warning signs of her unhappiness and eventual departure. Though I suspected there were differences between Paula and other members of the team, I just didn't know how bad they were. Because Paula didn't complain, I didn't feel that they were significant enough that I had to step in. I misjudged the situation and, as a result, I lost a valued employee. Leaders shouldn't have to wait until an employee decides to step forward and complain about a situation at work before they take action. Instead, leaders ought to keep an eye on things themselves without being told, asking questions before things spin out of control. I believe if I had done this myself, we would have kept Paula on our team instead of losing her. I regretted my oversight and was determined never to let this happen again. Good people are hard to find and wise leaders do everything they can to keep them happy and prevent them from leaving.

Talking to my friends and co-workers, I have found that "voting with your feet" is actually a very common phenomenon, one that every leader should be aware of. We shouldn't be satisfied simply with what our workers tell us, which may not always be honest and accurate. We should be looking for underlying issues or motivations that could drive our workers in a certain direction (or drive them out). The fact is, while some workers are very outspoken and more than glad to tell you exactly what is on their minds, they are often in the minority. Most workers don't want to have to speak up, preferring instead to keep quiet and eventually leaving rather than "rocking the boat". But when they do move on, the underlying issues often remain unaddressed, continuing to hamper the organization. Addressing the problem of "voting with your feet" doesn't just mean asking the deeper questions—it also requires that the leadership actually *care* about the concerns and be willing to take action to correct them.

Guiding Principle: Most workers are uncomfortable and unwilling to bring up issues that they see in the workplace and may be more likely to "vote with their feet" and leave the organization. A key reason for this reluctance is a perception that leadership is unwilling to listen or will not enact meaningful change based on the inputs they receive. Wise leaders will keep their eyes and ears open to any issues in the workplace and actively poll workers for any potential issues. When they get wind of them, they will aggressively work to correct issues, creating a culture that demonstrates that these types of inputs are welcome.

CHAPTER 37

Treating People Right

Years ago, I heard a story about a medical school professor who gave his students an exam. According to this story, the class participants, who were all excellent students, had carefully prepared for the test. That is, they were prepared for all the questions on the test except for the last one, which was 25 percent of the grade. The question simply said, "What is the name of our janitor, who empties the trash cans each day?"

After the test, in which everyone failed to answer that final question correctly, the students were irate. They argued with the instructor, claiming that the question was unfair and not relevant to the class. The instructor disagreed. You may believe that you are going into the medical field, he shared with them, where your job is simply to diagnose and heal people. What you may not realize, he continued, is that you are also going into the "people business", where everyone you encounter is a real person with very real hopes, fears, dreams, and concerns. You need to see these patients first and foremost as people and develop the skills to deal with them interpersonally and see them as real living and breathing individuals who matter, in addition to evaluating their medical issues. If you don't realize that you are actually going into the "people business", he concluded, you will never be a very good doctor.

I never forgot this story and the lesson it conveyed. It also made me think about myself and my own work. Like the medical field, the engineering and the spaceflight business seem like a purely technical field. Or so I thought. I quickly learned that it is a "people business" as well, I just didn't realize it at first. We deal with all sorts of people all the time, often working very closely with them and having to interact with others on a continual basis. How we treat and interact with people, even in our highly technical field, makes a huge difference in the success and failure of our technical work. Good interpersonal and communication skills help us to overcome difficult challenges by allowing us to work together to find solutions. On the other hand, poor interpersonal and communication skills can cause even minor problems to grow quickly into major obstacles.

Many people in the engineering and spaceflight field would maintain that, in our highly technical field, the way we treat people is not as important as the way we deal with facts, figures, and numbers. I believe this is completely wrong and an example of misguided thinking. The way we treat people matters—every time I feel that I have been treated poorly, it affects my performance and motivation and has even caused me to leave a project. Talking to my co-workers (all engineers, like me), I have seen that the same is true for others. Even at NASA, where we work with fielding advanced technologies to launch groundbreaking missions, we are still essentially in the "people business". As I look around our missions, the only pathway for all this advanced work to get done is through—you guessed it—people! As a result, we see time and time again that the way we treat people matters. It matters because we need to know how to motivate and get the best work out of people—even the most cynical and manipulative person knows that. I have found that, after many years of working alongside countless people, the "Golden Rule" is still the best workplace approach, which is treating others as you would like to be treated. The way we treat people also speaks volumes about us and the type of person we are.

Unless you work totally alone and do not interact with others, you are likely in a "people business" as well, though you may just not realize it. The most successful people in their fields *do* realize this and work to cultivate skills that help them navigate the "people" aspect of their business. A core skill in navigating interpersonal relationships is treating people with respect, kindness, and dignity, no matter who they are. Most people are nice to the people they work for, those who have control over their future and their fate, whether we actually like them or not. Frankly, it could be "career limiting" to be rude or disrespectful to such people. The real question, however, is how nice are we to our peers, or even to those who work under us? I have learned over the years that how we treat such people says the most about what kind of person we really are. The humorist Dave Barry put it best—"A person who is nice to you, but rude to the waiter, is not a nice person." All people are deserving of dignity, respect, and kindness, not just those who we deem important or those who have some sort of sway or control over our lives.

People matter, and treating people right is also good business. From a practical perspective, you never know who you might be dealing with. If you're not careful, you may find yourself ignoring or being rude to the wrong person and regretting it later. I remember being on a formal review panel for a high-profile mission proposal that was still working out the final kinks before its final submission. As a result, there were a lot of areas that needed a good polishing, and I had lots of questions and comments. I was engaging in a great deal of back-and-forth with the project proposal team who were presenting from the front of the room, all dressed formally in suits and ties. However, there were two very casually dressed guys sitting in the back of the room who kept interrupting our technical interchange, constantly cutting in and asking questions or requesting clarification. It was a bit distracting, but I worked hard to treat them with the same respect and courtesy as I did the project team at the front of the room. After a few hours of this, we finally took a break, and these two fellows came up to chat with me. To my surprise, the two casually dressed men were actually the lead scientists in charge of formulating and guiding the mission, and the entire project team in the room worked for them! We had a great conversation, and they thanked me profusely for my input, which they valued greatly. Ultimately, they offered me a job on the mission, which I turned down because I was already committed to a project. Just imagine, however, how the conversation would have gone differently if I hadn't given them the same respect as the well-dressed people I thought were in charge.

Most people want to work for those who treat others with respect and dignity. The average worker will figure out very quickly if you are genuinely a nice person or someone who picks and chooses only to be nice to the "important" ones.

Guiding Principle: People matter. How we treat people, whether they are our bosses or the individual who empties the trash in our office, speaks volumes about the type of person we are. In fact, a

huge measure of the type of person we really are is how we treat people who we don't have to be nice to. Wise leaders make a point of treating everyone with respect and dignity, not just because it is a good business and leadership practice, but because it is the right thing to do.

CHAPTER 38

Being a Lifelong Learner

This is a tale of two men. While to the casual observer, they might seem very similar, there was one major distinction between the two of them. That distinction made all the difference in their future paths and their success in the workplace.

Stan, who I once worked alongside, seemed on the surface to be the perfect employee, someone anyone would want on their team. He was smart, he had years of experience, and he demonstrated good leadership skills. On paper, his resume looked wonderful. There was just one problem. He knew everything.

He didn't, of course, but he thought he did. That one flaw proved, over time, to be a huge problem. When people tried to explain things to him, Stan would resist any explanation that remotely suggested that he had something to learn. I'm not sure if it was ego or insecurity or something else, but there was something in his psyche that wouldn't let him admit that there was something that he could possibly learn from other people. As a result, it was almost impossible to teach him anything new or for him to learn anything new from others. Because of this, his learning and personal growth seemed to just stop. It became a significant challenge just to work with him.

I also worked alongside another man. He was also smart, he also had years of experience, and he also demonstrated good leadership skills. This man was named Mike, who later became a trusted mentor of mine. The difference between Mike and Stan was that, at his core, Mike was a lifelong learner. He learned from everyone, and I mean *everyone*. He had an insatiable hunger to learn and was willing to learn from anyone who could teach him something. He was just as comfortable sitting down and talking for hours with an internationally renowned scientist as he was with the electrical technicians who worked anonymously in the labs, as long as they could teach him something. As a result, he knew a lot. Mike constantly amazed me with the depth and breadth of his knowledge in a myriad of areas. He was one of the smartest and most knowledgeable people I knew.

Sadly, Stan fell off my radar. When I think of him, he serves as a cautionary tale of lost potential. He never really made a big impact, as his "know-it-all" attitude seemed to constantly get in the way. Mike, on the other hand, had his career take off. He became highly sought after and was pressed into service to help out with one problem after another across NASA. The variety of things he got involved with covered a wide range of topics and technical areas, with Mike relishing the opportunity to learn something new in each. It didn't matter what the topic was; Mike would dig in with his characteristic vigor and learn all there was from whoever he could. After helping to solve it, he would move on to learn from the next problem.

To be fair, there were probably other differences between these two men that would explain why one became wildly successful and the other didn't. However, the one characteristic that clearly differentiated the two of them was a willingness to be a learner and to learn from others.

There is a false way of thinking that leads many people in the workplace astray. We've alluded to it a couple of times already in these pages. Some people think that it is very important to project that image that they are very knowledgeable and don't have much to learn. They believe that admitting that they don't know something demonstrates weakness. This is very wrong and can be very dangerous. In fact, it is actually a sign of insecurity and weakness itself. On the other hand, I have discovered that the more knowledgeable an individual is, the more they realize how much they *don't* know and they are much more willing to acknowledge this so that they can grow even more in their quest for knowledge and understanding.

No one knows everything. There is so much we can pick up from other people if we are just willing to listen and learn from them. This should be obvious, but you would be surprised how often the inability to learn from others seems to get in the way. When I am teaching a class to younger engineers, I always stress to them the importance of learning from others instead of learning only from one's own mistakes.

One of the best ways to reduce the number of mistakes is to learn from the mistakes of others. In the class, I would regularly urge rising engineers to adopt this mindset. To make this point, I would tell them the same thing that I have repeated many times to my own children—"A stupid person doesn't learn from their mistakes and is doomed to repeat them. A smart person *does* learn from their mistakes and doesn't repeat them again. However, a *wise* person learns from *other* people's mistakes, learning from others' missteps and avoiding making them on their own." There are many experienced people out there who would gladly be willing to pass on their lessons-learned. This can save you a lot of effort, a lot of heartache, and a lot of time. As Eleanor Roosevelt once said, "Learn from the mistakes of others. You can't live long enough to make them all yourself." Or, as a friend once told me, "If you don't get older and wiser, then you just get older."

It's probably a good idea to accept now that you're never going to arrive at that elusive place where you know it all. If you're willing to accept this, it's time to adopt the posture of a "lifelong learner". Once you do this, you'll be open to learning a lot more, and, at the same time, you'll likely be opening the door to a successful future.

Guiding Principle: No one knows everything. There are people all around us who have wisdom and experience to share as long as we are willing to listen. Wise leaders adopt the attitude of "lifelong learners", learning from the mistakes and lessons-learned of others rather than having to repeat them themselves.

CHAPTER 39

The Value of Experience

Early in my career at NASA, I worked alongside Bob, who was by all accounts an excellent engineer. We both held similar jobs on the same project and he was very helpful to me since he had worked at NASA longer than I did. I would often go to him as I was learning the ropes, and he would fill in the gaps on the many, many things about working at NASA that I didn't understand.

Over time, however, something started to bother me. Where I was always running around, worrying about everything, Bob seemed as cool as a cucumber. In fact, he never seemed to worry about anything. While I was often frantic, I sometimes wondered if Bob was even paying attention. After seeing this pattern continue for some time, my high opinion of Bob started to diminish. I even wondered if he was fully aware of what was going on around him on the project, or even if he was as committed to the mission as I was.

Although it took me a while, I finally figured out what was going on. Bob had something that I didn't have and it made all the difference between us. What Bob had that I was missing was *experience*. What I didn't realize at the time was that Bob had already worked on a flight project, while this was my first time into the breach. I suspect that on his first time through Bob had been just as frantic as I was, trying to juggle everything at once and trying to figure out what was important, what needed to be done now, and what could wait until later. After completing a mission for the first time through, he had learned a great deal about how things were done and what should be prioritized. On his second mission, he was now applying this experience to inform his decision-making and prioritization process. On the other hand, I did not have this experience and was always frantically trying to figure everything out real time, struggling to discern what should be prioritized over other things. That real-world experience made all the difference between us and how we were able to perform on the project.

This was my first real exposure to the true value of experience. Experience is not, as some people may believe, primarily for boasting about how much you know. This is a common workplace misperception. Instead, experience provides a practical and effective way to better understand the work in front of you, prioritize tasks based on their relative importance, and effectively apply resources to get this work done in the most efficient and successful manner possible. Experience allows us to use the lessons learned from our previous work to better focus on what is important, teaching us what to worry about and when. This fact-based understanding allows its holder to prioritize tasks and, in some cases, ignore them altogether. Alternatively, someone unburdened by experience is forced to worry about all items equally for fear of letting something important fall through the cracks. As a result, experience can be a huge force multiplier for someone who is facing a large number of things on their plate, allowing them to intelligently pick and choose what needs to be done and when. The reason that Bob was able to be better focused and less stressed than me was not necessarily because he was smarter or harder working than I was—it was because he had experience on his side informing his decision process and I did not.

Experience is, at its core, all about learning by doing. There's only one way to get experience, and you can't get it any faster no matter how hard you try. As we actually do things, we learn from our successes and failures and they inform our thinking and our understanding of how things get done. A truly successful individual will allow successive experiences to build on one another and create a body of practical knowledge and expertise. This is one of the reasons that people and organizations place great stock in the number of years of experience an individual has in a specific area. The assumption is that the number of years of experience directly corresponds to a constant practice of learning by doing, then reapplying these lessons back into the workplace. The years of experience imply a greater degree of hands-on understanding and proficiency, thereby obtaining a greater mastery in an area that they can apply to their work.

I have worked on projects with people who had previous experience in what we were attempting to accomplish and have been amazed at how their experience-based understanding streamlined our work. They seemed to know what to do and in what order, what was important and needed to be done, and what could be discarded or ignored. If an individual were to make similar assumptions without the commensurate experience, their actions would likely be guesswork and would be very risky and dangerous.

I've seen the value of experience in my own work history. As I mentioned earlier, at the beginning of my career, I was overwhelmed with all that was on my plate. There were innumerable things to worry about and I didn't understand how to prioritize them and therefore treated them all equally. My efforts in trying to keep up with everything on my plate proved to be exhausting. Later, as I gained more experience, I realized that certain things were more important than others, and started developing an experience-based hierarchy of priorities that I could apply to my work. No longer were all tasks "flat" or equal in importance—now some tasks were clearly more important than others, greatly assisting me in organizing my work against my limited resources. Over time, as my experience grew, I learned how to instinctively organize and prioritize tasks based on what I had learned from previous work. My efficiency and effectiveness were multiplied significantly, and I was able to direct others as well, rather than simply doing work myself. My hard-won experience base served as a huge force multiplier for both me and my team.

It would be wonderful if we could somehow inject ourselves with the experience of others, thereby shortcutting the process of gaining this hard-won expertise. But experience can only be gained one way—by doing and learning on our own. Experience, coupled with mentoring and wisdom passed on from others, is an effective tool in effectively prioritizing work, allowing workers to both intelligently decide what tasks need to be done and when, as well as how to complete them successfully.

Guiding Principle: Experience is practical expertise that can only be gained by doing things on your own. Experience tells its holder

what is important and what matters, allowing them to prioritize activities and providing practical lessons that lead to successful completion of tasks. A wise leader will work hard to gain experience, which serves as a force multiplier not only in their own work, but also in guiding the work of those working under them.

CHAPTER 40

Avoiding Communication Missteps

It was supposed to be a simple e-mail to the team, covering a variety of topics. I could have called a team meeting, but I decided instead to send out an e-mail to the group and did so quickly before going to bed. It was simple, straightforward, and uncontroversial (or so I thought). I closed it out by encouraging anyone who had questions to e-mail me back or give me a call. I sent the e-mail from home, late at night, then shut down my computer and went to bed, unaware of what was coming.

The next day, once I got into my office, a phonemail message was awaiting me. It was Kevin, a valued and productive member of my team. And he wasn't happy. In fact, he was furious. He had left a long, ranting message on my phonemail, hopping mad, and on the verge of yelling. It took me a few times listening to the message to figure out what he was mad about. Finally, I figured it out. It was my (seemingly innocuous) e-mail from the night before.

Kevin had somehow seized on one of my comments in the e-mail, interpreted it out of context, saw it as a criticism of him, and let me have it. In reality, I was saying nothing of the kind. I valued Kevin immensely. However, a rushed late-day e-mail with some poor word choice on my part, coupled with Kevin's overly negative and out-of-context interpretation, created a perfect storm to set Kevin on fire. We met later that day, and, after a long conversation, we worked it out. I apologized for my poor and confusing wording and Kevin hung his head and apologized for overreacting and losing his temper. This episode was another cautionary reminder of the dangers of e-mail and what a poor communication tool it can be.

I share this story because this type of disconnect and subsequent blowup is not an isolated instance, but rather is an all-too-common workplace occurrence. It serves as a warning of the dangers of communication failures, often through mediums like e-mail and texting where limited information is shared and can be easily misconstrued, with negative results. A seemingly innocuous exchange, either poorly written or misconstrued by the recipient, can set in motion a significant communication snafu and a major misunderstanding.

In our increasingly networked workplace, more and more communication takes place via e-mail rather than face-to-face meetings. We're told that e-mail messages are just as clear and effective as face-to-face communication. Spoiler alert—they're not. As with all tools, e-mail has areas where it is extremely useful and areas where it is not.

I'm old enough to remember the days in the workplace before e-mail existed, and what a novelty it was when it was first introduced (Yes, I realize that I'm dating myself). Since that time, it has proven to be an amazing communication tool and has helped tremendously in connecting people and disseminating information. At the same time, its misuse has also created conflict and misunderstanding in the workplace. Used properly, it is a useful tool. When not used with care, it can cause lots of problems.

E-mail is just a tool and as such is "value neutral"—it is in itself neither good nor bad. Like any other tool, it is important to understand the ways where it can be used effectively and the ways where its use can cause problems. I would strongly recommend seeking out tips on e-mail etiquette or taking measures such as proofreading before sending, or even waiting a period of time before sending an e-mail that might be inflammatory. As a real-life example of this last item, I can recall a time when I was incredibly annoyed at a co-worker and was angrily drafting an e-mail on my keyboard when my deputy project manager walked by my office door. Seeing my furious pounding on the keyboard, she stopped and simply said, "Whatever email you are writing, wait and send it tomorrow." I wisely took her advice, waiting until the next day to review it in the light of a new day. With a fresh set of eyes, I realized the e-mail was too inflammatory and would have not helped the situation, and promptly deleted it.

After numerous missteps and mistakes over the years, I have learned that e-mail is a very useful tool for passing along information, facts, and data, but is often terrible for anything personal, controversial, or just about anything that can be misinterpreted. The reason for this is that e-mail (and its sisters, texting and social media) does an extremely poor job of conveying tone and emotion, which we use in interpreting language and its meaning.

One of the advantages of e-mail is its asynchronous communication method (communication that does not take place in real-time), making it excellent for leaving messages that the recipient can read and respond to later at their leisure. Face-to-face contact is not required, perfect for leaving messages that can be sent anytime to be answered later. However, this is where its chief drawback emerges as well. In normal real-time face-to-face communications, any misunderstandings can be quickly corrected and any disagreement smoothed over. However, the time lag in-between e-mail exchanges and the limited information contained in e-mail creates a fertile ground for miscommunication and misunderstandings to flourish. There is no real-time feedback and correction loop. Disconnects that would be quickly addressed face-to-face instead have the opportunity to fester and grow, allowing them to become real issues and potentially growing out of control.

Another problem with e-mail is that the recipient can zero in and focus exclusively on specific passages in an e-mail and ignore the larger message and its context. Again, with no real-time correction, any out-of-context assumptions or misrepresentations can go uncorrected over time and grow from what should have been a harmless misunderstanding to a major negative event. In my e-mail to Kevin, a poorly written snippet of an e-mail captured his attention while he missed the larger message and context of the overall e-mail, and there was no real-time correction and re-direction to the larger message as can take place in real-time conversations.

I have also observed that people will often say things in an e-mail that they would never say face-to-face to another person. I suspect there is something about the anonymity of sitting behind a computer screen that causes people to write things that they would never say face-to-face.

A great example of this is an e-mail that Brian, a good friend of mine, received from one of his workers. Something had happened to set this man off and, that night (it always seems to be at night!), he sent out a nasty e-mail to Brian. The e-mail was inflammatory, rude, and abusive. Rather than respond in kind, Brian instead contacted this employee and asked him to meet in his office early the next morning. The next day, the disgruntled employee showed up at his office, still angry but likely realizing that he was about to be disciplined. Rather than showing any repentance, he came ready to fight. Brian had him sit and addressed his e-mail, saying that he had received it the previous evening and was confused. When the other man started to wind up for an argument, Brian raised his hand and asked him to stop. Again, he stated that he was confused by the e-mail and didn't understand what the other man was trying to say. He reached over and handed the man a printed copy of the e-mail and asked him to read it aloud. The man, a bit taken aback, took the e-mail and began to read aloud. One paragraph in, after reading out loud the abusive text of his message, he stopped, took a deep breath, and apologized.

What Brian realized, and what most of us forget, is that people will often write things down that they would *never* say aloud. When we are behind our computer screens, we are often much more willing to say things that we would never say face-to-face. By asking this man to read what he had written, he allowed the man to take a step back and repeat, in person and face-to-face, what he had previously hidden behind an e-mail to say. In the light of day, in front of a living, breathing person, what he had written while safely ensconced behind a computer terminal suddenly didn't seem like a good idea. Brian then used the opportunity to address his issues calmly and they parted that day on good terms.

It all comes down to how we use e-mail as to whether it is a curse or blessing. Passing along information, instructions, and data is a very useful application for e-mail. It is not a good workplace medium for communicating anything personal, controversial, or that can be misinterpreted. It should only be used for these types of communication if there are no other reasonable alternatives, and, even in those cases, the e-mail should be carefully reviewed for possible unintended effects or misunderstandings before sending. For example, we've all heard horror stories (and rolled our eyes when hearing them) of people who have been fired by e-mail, text, or social media. We *know* that this is wrong, no one has to tell us this. Why? Because we know that some interactions require face-to-face communication due to their importance, gravity, or sensitivity, as uncomfortable as they may be. These types of communications are important enough that it is not the time to sacrifice interpersonal communication for efficiency.

Whenever I get the impression e-mail conversation may be leading to a misunderstanding, I immediately suggest a phone call or, better yet, a face-to-face conversation if they are close by. Almost every time I have departed from this approach, I have regretted it. Too many times, I have sat down at my computer, thinking "I'll smooth this issue over with a quick explanatory email." Sadly, that almost *never* happens. It has taken me a long time to learn that e-mail is a horrible communication tool for anything except for information and data. When it comes to communicating any sort of emotion or smoothing over problems, it fails miserably. Your best bet is to have as close to a face-to-face meeting that you can. If the person you are communicating with is local, meet with them and do it fast. If they are not local, call them or set up a teleconference. The more they can see your face and gauge your body language (and you theirs) the better, and the more likely you will be able to connect with them to dispel any emerging disagreement and get on the same page.

We have said that communication is a vital aspect of any successful endeavor (see **"A Failure to Communicate"**). But *how* you communicate is pivotal and can also make the difference between success and failure. We should use all the communication forms that are available to us. Sometimes e-mail is the best and most efficient way to communicate and pass on information, and sometimes it is the worst. It all comes down to how we use e-mail (and its sisters, texting and social media), as to whether it is a curse or a blessing.

Guiding Principle: Communication is essential for a smooth running and successful team, but all modes of communication are not equal—each has its benefits and disadvantages. In the

modern workplace, e-mail is widely used but can result in misunderstandings and potential conflicts if the sender and recipient are not careful. Wise leaders will take care to carefully choose which medium they use for different types of communications.

CHAPTER 41

The Value of Relationships

Sometimes, despite our best planning and preparation, problems still arise that can create serious setbacks. That's where we found ourselves in building our flight hardware for one of our missions. Although my team designs the flight boards and procures the flight parts that populate them, we typically employ an experienced manufacturing company to actually assemble the flight boards. These manufacturing vendors have the dedicated infrastructure, people, and experience to do this type of work better than we can, and are able to handle a greater volume of work than we could do ourselves. After receiving the completed flight boards, our team tests and debugs these electronics boards before integrating and testing them as completed flight avionics units. Knowing that sometimes these facilities have many customers and that logjams can sometimes occur, we had planned well ahead to make sure our hardware would have clear sailing through the facility.

Or so we thought. Unfortunately, as things often happen, problems and other priorities at the vendor's facility resulted in scheduling issues anyway. As a result, our team was looking at manufacturing delays that would seriously impact our schedule. I worked with our contacts at the company, desperate to see if there was anything we could do to reset their priorities and regain our schedule. They worked hard to help us, but ultimately came back and let us know that their hands were tied and that there was nothing they could do.

After thinking this over, on a whim I called Joseph, who also worked at the company and who I knew quite well. We had worked together on a previous mission, with him overseeing our flight hardware manufacturing. We had developed a good working relationship, finding ways to help each other out, overcome problems, and work through red tape. The mission had been successful, and Joseph's assistance to us had been a significant part of it. As a result of his excellent work on our and other missions, he had been promoted into a more senior leadership position in the company, which he deserved. We had stayed in touch, although infrequently, and I decided to give him a call. I explained our situation to him and asked him if there was anything he could do to help us out —if not, I would completely understand. Joseph listened carefully and told me he couldn't make any promises, but he would look into it and see what he could. After a few days, he called me back. He had been able to work with the organization and, while he couldn't give us everything we wanted, he was able to redirect resources and provide substantial schedule relief, helping us immensely. I thanked him profusely and told him that I owed him one.

Please note what I *didn't* do here. I didn't bully, threaten, or cajole to try to get what I wanted. There's a popular workplace ideology that suggests that coming in forcefully, like a bull in a china shop, is the most effective way to plow through problems and get what you need. I believe this approach is wrong and unhelpful. I don't like working that way and I don't think it's professional or fruitful. However, what I *did* do was reach out to someone who I had a good working relationship with, explain our problem, and ask if there was anything he could do to help us out. Because of our good working relationship, he went the extra mile and was able to pull some strings to provide the relief I needed. This is a clear example of the value of positive relationships within a workplace environment.

One of the best ways to build these types of positive relationships with others is by simply working with them. As part of our normal workplace interactions, these types of lasting and effective relationships are created and developed naturally over time. Of course, this is predicated on the fact that your work interactions with other people are seen as positive, and they look back on them favorably. When you interact with people, do they leave with a favorable impression of you? Or are they secretly glad when they don't have to deal with you any longer? As always, how we treat people matters and leaves a lasting impression.

Even in a technical field, which is not known for complex interpersonal interactions, building positive working relationships between parties has a huge benefit. It creates trust, promotes understanding, and helps build bridges over any disconnects and disagreements that can crop up in a workplace setting. Positive working relationships help the other team feel valued and go a long way to help create an actual partnership rather than an employer–client relationship

Never underestimate the value of a positive working relationship in smoothing over the issues and disconnects that invariably occur in our daily workplace. A friend of mine once wisely told me "In the absence of a positive relationship, even minor disconnects are often greeted with suspicion and distrust." Positive working relationships naturally affect the working environment, as well as serve as an effective buffer against misunderstandings and potential conflicts.

I find it humorous that, in talking about the NASA workplace, a *highly* technical workplace environment, we are once again talking about "the value of relationships". This serves as another reminder that, even in the most technical of areas, we are still dealing with people and how they interact, and that we are never going to get away from addressing "people issues" unless individuals work completely by themselves, isolated from the outside world. The better people are in building positive relationships, the more success they will have in navigating these "people issues".

It's worth noting that face-to-face communications are a vital component in building the type of effective working relationships that we have been discussing. Very rarely are these types of strong relationships built solely over e-mail, and even via teleconference and video links. There is something about face-to-face communications and the natural interactions and "hallway conversations" that they afford that are very effective in building relationships. This is why, on our NASA missions, we hold regular site visits with all of our key vendors—in some cases, we visit them quarterly. While there certainly are technical interchanges accomplished during these visits, much of this could just as easily be accomplished via teleconference or phone meetings. However, wise leaders recognize the relationship-building value of these meetings, allowing working teams to meet and get to know each other and building bridges that will pay dividends later in the working relationship. Sometimes, the most effective parts of the meetings are during the "down time" in between meetings, where frank, honest, and private conversations can be held.

The idea of the value of these face-to-face interactions was certainly challenged during the COVID lockdowns, where our mission team was forced to develop our mission concept while our team was working remotely during the pandemic. This remote work environment removed the opportunity for face-to-face meetings and, as a result, significantly curtailed aspects of relationship building that in-person meetings afforded. While we were still able to work and develop our mission concept remotely, there is no question that our team and our partners were hampered due to the lack of face-to-face contact we normally relied upon to help conduct our work. Relationship building during this time certainly suffered. Minor differences and disconnects that would have easily been addressed and disposed of in between meetings lingered longer than necessary and, in some cases, created team issues.

Finally, I'm reminded of what someone told me years ago about the secret to winning at the game of Monopoly. While playing Monopoly does require some skill and certainly some luck to land on the right locations on the board, there is a clear strategy that defines more often than not who will win the game. The secret to winning at Monopoly is being the person in the game who is most likable and the one that most of the other players least mind losing to. Monopoly is, at its core, a game of deals and trading properties, which is essential to building a portfolio that will allow you to ultimately win the game. If people like you (or at least dislike you less than the others), this means that they are more likely to trade with you than with others, making it more likely that you will win. In the same way, building positive working relationships with others makes it more likely that they will be willing to make compromises and work with you to get to a positive outcome. Conversely, a negative working relationship likely decreases your chances of others bending over backward to help you.

Taking the time to build positive working relationships can be of tremendous benefit in a workplace environment. Such relationships can go a long way in building strong partnerships both within and outside of a team. They promote goodwill, understanding, trust, and a shared purpose that creates valuable partnerships and helps overcome any organizational or communication disconnects and obstacles.

Guiding Principle: Building positive working relationships is a key ingredient in successful partnerships within a team and with outside organizations. It promotes understanding, creates trust, and is a huge advantage in bridging any issues or disconnects that inevitably arise in any working relationship. These types of positive relationships should be a natural byproduct of a respectful and gracious teaming environment, creating an environment where all parties work together in partnership toward mission success.

CHAPTER 42

Next Steps

In my job as a mission systems engineer leading various flight projects, whenever I wrapped up a major review or discussion of a technical challenge we were looking to solve, I would always end by putting up a final slide titled, "*Next Steps*". The point I was trying to make was that we were not done ... yet. Even though we knew the path forward, understood the obstacles in front of us, and were ready to continue, there was recognition that we were not yet finished, that there was still a lot of roadway ahead of us that needed to be traversed before we would reach the end. I wanted everyone to know—our reviewers, our team, and myself as well—we knew that we had work in front of us and that we would not rest on our laurels until it was completed.

The contents of this book are no different. Hopefully, as you read through these pages, you saw some things that challenged you, there was recognition of areas where some changes and improvements might be needed, and you saw that there was still a lot of roadway ahead of you that needed traveling. It is my hope that you jotted down some "next steps" that you might want to take as a result of reading these pages.

I have an admission for you—I have not "arrived" yet either. As I documented these "lessons learned", it's clear that I still have a significant roadway to travel on my own and that there are some areas that I still need to work on. I think that is the nature of pursuing excellence in work and in life—we never "arrive", but we continue to learn and grow along the way. I hope in my pursuit of being a "lifelong learner" that I will never rest on my laurels but will constantly try to grow and learn until my last breath. I hope that I will always realize that I am not done ... yet.

It is my hope that these hard-won lessons from my own work experience and life have been helpful to you. I wish you the best on your path forward in pursuing excellence and personal growth, and that any helpful suggestions you glean from these pages benefit not only you but the people you work with and those you walk alongside in life.

About the Author

During his career as a NASA engineer, **John Ruffa** led the technical development of multiple NASA spaceflight missions. John leverages this practical, hands-on experience to clearly identify the lies and mistruths prevalent in today's workforce and the skills needed to help workers navigate complex workplace environments.

Index

Barry, D., 198–199
Big picture, 171–175
Blind spots, 123–127
Boots-on-the-ground perspective, 69, 70
Burnout, 181–185

Clance, P. R., 113–114
Communication
    face-to-face, 210–213, 217–218
    failure, 23–27
    misunderstandings, 209–214
Community building, 19–22
Critical Design Review (CDR), 143–144

Descartes, R., 141
The Dropout (TV series), 120

E-mail, 209–214
Experience, value of, 205–208

Face-to-face communication, 210–213, 217–218
Failure
    communication, 23–27
    recovering from, 143–149
Fear-based management approach, 156
Fear-based philosophy, 155–156
Fear *vs.* loyalty, 155–159
Feedback, 74–75, 116–117, 125–127

Goddard rules, 138, 140
Golden Rule, 158, 198
Groupthink, 83–86

Hard skills, 13–17
Hawking, S., 172
Holmes, E., 120, 121

Imes, S., 113–114
Impostor syndrome, 113–117
Insular leadership approach, 74

Janis, I., 83

Kindergartener-tested approach, 153

Leadership, 2–5, 26–27, 50, 57, 67–68, 70, 72–79, 109, 111, 115–117, 123–127, 156, 163–165, 193–195
Lifelong learner, 201–203
Loyalty, fear *vs.*, 155–159

MacArthur, D., 137
Mentoring relationship, 31–35, 39
Mentor/mentoring, 37–40
Mentor value, 29–35
Miscommunication. *See* Communication

Negotiation, 151–154
Networking issue, 88
Not invented here culture, 88–89

People matter, 197–200
People-type issues, 10–13, 15–17, 89
Peter Principle, 56
Potential mentor, 34, 38
Preliminary Design Review (PDR), 143–144

Reinventing the wheel trap, 87–90
Risk Management, 133–136

Sink-or-swim approach, 55
Soft skills, 13–17
Space Shuttle Challenger (1986), 83

Team culture, 77–81
Technical *vs.* nontechnical challenges, 9–12
Theranos, 120, 121
Train-your-replacement mentality, 95–99

Weiler, E., 103

Wilkinson Microwave Anisotropy Probe (WMAP), 171–172, 174
Workplace lies, 1–8
Worry, 129–132
Wren, C., 172–173

X-Ray Timing Explorer, 43

OTHER TITLES IN THE HUMAN RESOURCE MANAGEMENT AND ORGANIZATIONAL BEHAVIOR COLLECTION

Michael J. Provitera and Michael Edmondson, Editors

- *The Negotiation Edge* by Michael Saksa
- *Applied Leadership* by Sam Altawil
- *Forging Dynasty Businesses* by Chuck Violand
- *How the Harvard Business School Changed the Way We View Organizations* by Jay W. Lorsch
- *Managing Millennials* by Jacqueline Cripps
- *Personal Effectiveness* by Lucia Strazzeri
- *Catalyzing Transformation* by Sandra Waddock
- *Critical Leadership and Management Tools for Contemporary Organizations* by Tony Miller
- *Leading From the Top* by Dennis M. Powell
- *Warp Speed Habits* by Marco Neves
- *I Don't Understand* by Buki Mosaku
- *Nurturing Equanimity* by Michael Edmondson
- *Speaking Up at Work* by Ryan E. Smerek
- *Living a Leadership Lifestyle* by Ross Emerson
- *Business Foresight* by Tony Grundy

Concise and Applied Business Books

The Collection listed above is one of 30 business subject collections that Business Expert Press has grown to make BEP a premiere publisher of print and digital books. Our concise and applied books are for…

- Professionals and Practitioners
- Faculty who adopt our books for courses
- Librarians who know that BEP's Digital Libraries are a unique way to offer students ebooks to download, not restricted with any digital rights management
- Executive Training Course Leaders
- Business Seminar Organizers

Business Expert Press books are for anyone who needs to dig deeper on business ideas, goals, and solutions to everyday problems. Whether one print book, one ebook, or buying a digital library of 110 ebooks, we remain the affordable and smart way to be business smart. For more information, please visit www.businessexpertpress.com, or contact sales@businessexpertpress.com.

www.ingramcontent.com/pod-product-compliance
Lightning Source LLC
Chambersburg PA
CBHW071142120225
21824CB00014B/69